To Ilaria, a rare friend

Published in the United States in 1999 by
Contemporary Books
A division of NTC/Contemporary Publishing
Group, Inc.
4255 West Touhy Avenue
Lincolnwood (Chicago), Illinois 60646-1975 U.S.A.

ISBN 0-0892-2667-7

Commissioning Editor Suzannah Gough
Managing Editor Kate Bell
Editorial Assistant Tanya Robinson
Copy Editor Norma MacMillan

Art Director Leslie Harrington
Art Editor Alison Fenton
Stylist Wei Tang
Food for Photography Meg Jansz
Typesetting Olivia Norton

Picture Research Rachel Davies
Production Julian Deeming

Cataloging-in-Publication Data is available from the
United States Library of Congress
Printed and bound in China by Toppan

Page 1 *Couscous with Seven Vegetables (page 78)*
Pages 2–3 *Pomegranate Juice (page 121)*
Pages 4–5 *Mussels with Tomatoes and Coriander (page 51)*

café

morocco

Anissa Helou

Photography by Jeremy Hopley

CONTEMPORARY BOOKS

Contents

Introduction

When people in the West talk about "street food," they usually mean fast food: hot dogs or hamburgers in America (and all over the world now), fish and chips in England, *baguette* sandwiches in France, or raw marinated fish in Holland, to name but a few examples. All are ready in minutes, to be eaten as we rush about.

In Morocco, street food is different. The choice is much more varied and the ingredients are rarely processed. Almost all the food is produced on a small scale. There just isn't any of the mass production of fast-food products that we know in the West. People eat on the streets because of necessity rather than laziness or greed, and they expect the food to be similar to that in their homes. Travelers, *souk*-traders, and shoppers all go to the tiny food stalls and cafés of the *medinas* to eat breakfast, lunch, or dinner. Quite often there is only space for one long table where they will sit *côte à côte* (rib to rib) with total strangers, but, Moroccans being a friendly people, it is not long before conversations are started. If they are at daily *souks* or at fairs (*mawassems*), they would buy fresh ingredients from the nearby greengrocers and butchers and take them to one of the cookshops, set up in makeshift tents, for the cook to prepare them a tagine (stew). The only difference between the food they will eat on the streets and that at home is that the former will be cooked by men and the latter by women.

If you were to walk through the bustling *medinas* in search of food, you would have to follow the pattern of daily meals consumed at home. The only stalls that will serve you early in the morning are those that provide breakfast fare: *beyssara* (dried fava beans stewed with cumin and paprika), lambs' heads and calves' feet (perhaps not everyone's idea of breakfast, but a definite favorite here), *rghayef* (flat breads), *beghrir* (pancakes), and, of course, Moroccan bread (*ksra*), a round, flattish loaf with a soft crust and a thick inside, which is best when made with whole-wheat flour; sometimes you will find it flavored with anise seed and sesame seeds.

Whole trussed lambs will be lowered and sealed into clay-pit ovens at 9:30 a.m.; three and a half hours later they will be hauled out and put on the slab, their golden skin glistening in the sun. The charcoal fires you will see burning in long rectangular metal braziers will be ready for the brochettes at midday—then, if you want to eat your brochettes as you walk about, the cooked meat will be slipped off the skewers into half a bread for you to take away and eat like a sandwich. Before then, at about 10:30 a.m., the tagines will be put to simmer in earthenware dishes of the same name, each over its own individual charcoal brazier. At lunchtime, the big pans of oil in which the fish is to be fried will be heated up, and the salads and fried vegetables will go on display.

From that time on you will be able to eat until the shops close at night and the *medinas* become deserted. In some places, like the area around the slaughterhouse in Casablanca, where they specialize in *mechoui* (roast whole lambs) and variety meats, street food is available until the early hours of the morning. It is there that the well-heeled *Casablancais* go for an early breakfast after a night out.

If you don't want a full street meal and only have room for a snack, you've got lots of choice. Throughout the day you will be able to buy scrumptious doughnuts (*sfinge*) that look like chunky golden bracelets; or nibble on grilled corn on the cob, dripping with salted water; or burn your palate eating a tiny bowl of snails simmered in a fiery, herb broth (you discard the gorgeous striped shells into a huge enamel bowl, wondering what will become of them); or stand by an egg cart, shelling hard-boiled eggs and dipping them in a mixture of salt and cumin before eating them; or crunch on crisp, savory or sweet pastries taken out of glass cabinets where they are kept away from flies.

The ultimate place to eat Moroccan street food is at Jame' el Fna, in Marrakesh, a square deserted during the day except for a few lone snake charmers and charlatan healers and a row of fresh fruit juice and nut sellers. All this changes after sunset, though, and the square comes to life. A whole army of ambulant food sellers moves in to set up a large rectangular formation of mobile restaurants, the cooks and food on the inside and the trestle tables and benches on the outside. It is one of the very few places where prices are written up on small boards. The stalls are grouped by specialty. You will spot the soup corner from the small plates of dates (a must with *harira*) set neatly on the tables awaiting customers. The adjacent variety-meats corner will either charm or repulse you, although the sight of baked lambs' heads grinning on the chopping boards, ready for their cheeks to be hacked off, always tickles me. Then there is what I call the miscellaneous corner, where bowls of steaming couscous, large round trays of turmeric-dyed yellow chickens, and platters of *salades variées*, fried eggplants and peppers, and fried fish are on offer. And, of course, there is a whole row of charcoal grills: meat and liver brochettes, *merguez* (spicy sausages), and *teyhan* (stuffed spleen), all served with the obligatory tomato and onion salad.

The following recipes represent a wide choice of Moroccan street food. Only a few of the typical dishes (snails, lambs' heads, etc.), which are too time-consuming to prepare or with ingredients that are hard to obtain, have not been included. I hope that when you try these at home you will be transported to the lively *medinas* and villages, or, if you have already been there, that they will evoke the smells and tastes of Morocco.

The Moroccan pantry

Almonds (loz) *Any pantry in Morocco, poor or rich, will have its ready supply of almonds, and in the pantries of the rich the almonds will be very large. Almonds are eaten fresh in early summer when in season, and are used in both savory and sweet dishes.*

Argan oil (zayt argan) *This is extracted from the fruit of the argan tree. The oil is produced with the help of goats. The goats eat the fruits, but as they cannot digest the pit they expel it, cleaned of any flesh. The pits are then picked up and broken, and the nuts taken out to be pressed like olives. The resulting oil has a delicate nutty taste, and is used in salads and in some sweets.*

Couscous (kseksü) *Couscous consists of tiny balls of semolina grain coated with a fine layer of flour. The semolina and flour are sprinkled with a little salted water as they are rolled with the palm of the hand against the sides of a wide, shallow straw bowl (midüna) to form the couscous balls. Couscous is Morocco's national dish, and Friday is the day when the whole nation sits down to a steaming couscous, with garnishes varying according to the household. Couscous is also always served at the end of a diffa (banquet), to make sure that no guests are left hungry. It comes in three grades: very fine, fine, and in small round pellets that are called* m'hamssa.

Crushed hot chili peppers (südaniyya) *In Morocco, a mixture of various types of dried hot chili peppers is used. These are ground to a coarse texture, similar to that of crushed dried herbs. Dried hot red pepper flakes make a good substitute.*

Dates (tamr) *A staple in the deserts of North Africa and Arabia. The Arabs believe that when God created the world, he formed the date-palm tree from the matter that was left over after making Adam. There are many varieties, but the California Medjool dates are the nearest to the fine ones from Tafilalt. Dates are used in tagines and in fish or game fillings.*

Green tea (atay akhdar) *Green tea from China or Japan is the one used for mint tea. Tea came into widespread use in Morocco in the middle of the nineteenth century, when English traders brought their tea loads to the trading posts of Tangiers and Mogador. Tea quickly became fashionable, and the Moroccans started adding it to the herbal infusions they were so fond of, most notably to mint.*

Herbs *Together with cilantro, parsley is the herb most used in Moroccan cooking. The flat-leaf variety is the one to use. Cilantro is related to parsley and both leaves and seeds (coriander) are used, though the latter less often. Mint is hardly ever used in cooking, but is essential for mint tea. A familiar sight in the souks of Morocco is stacks of large bunches of spearmint.*

Honey ('assal) *Sweet-spicy tagines are one of the most distinctive features of Moroccan cooking. The sweetness is usually achieved by adding honey or powdered sugar. The quality and flavor of the honey you use is important for the final taste and texture of the sauce.*

Mastic (meska) *Sometimes wrongly called gum arabic, mastic is an aromatic resin that exudes from open slits in the stems of plants of the genus* Pistacia. *The dried resin "tears" (or grains) are powdered before use. North Africans add mastic to savory dishes, whereas Arabs and Turks normally use it in sweets and ice creams. In Morocco, mastic is also used to flavor drinking water. Although not widely available in the U.S., it can usually be found in some ethnic or specialty food stores.*

Olives (zeytün) *Olives are a key ingredient or garnish of many Moroccan dishes. Those used most often are the fleshy purple ones. Greek or Spanish olives are a good substitute.*

Orange flower water (ma z'har) *This fragrant water is distilled from the flowers of the bitter Seville or bigarade orange. The flowers are picked in the* spring, spread on a sheet, and left in a sheltered place for 2 days before being distilled. It is used to flavor fruit juices and some sweet salads and tagines.

Preserved lemons (hamed makbüs) *Preserved lemons are a conspicuous taste in Moroccan food, and the most highly prized are the very small ones called* doqq. *When buying preserved lemons, make sure you select those that are preserved in salt only, without any untraditional ingredients such as pickling spice or garlic. They can also be made at home (see page 24).*

Prunes (barqüq) *Dried plums are used in only one dish, the famous Tagine of Lamb with Prunes (see page 64), which can also be prepared with chicken. It is found on almost every restaurant menu in Morocco, but is eaten less frequently on the streets unless you take the ingredients to a "cook shop" and ask them to make it for you.*

Purslane (rijla) *An ancient plant that has been eaten for 2000 years, purslane was called "the blessed vegetable" by the Arabs. Its fleshy, oval leaves are cooked to make a summer version of* baqüla *(see page 96) or used raw in some salads. Purslane can be found in Middle Eastern markets in the summer.*

Ras el hanout *This is a mixture of nearly 30 different spices, including various hot chilies, dried roses, the*

aphrodisiac Spanish fly (for use of which the Marquis de Sade ended up in prison), cardamom, cloves, turmeric, cinnamon, and ginger. It is added to some sweet-spicy tagines, game dishes, and kefta (see page 54). In winter, people use it to make an infusion to cure colds. Ras el hanout means "head of the shop," reflecting the value of its preparation. The composition varies from one spice merchant to another, and it is sold both in ground form and with the spices left whole.

Saffron (za'faran el horr) *The dried stigmas of* Crocus sativus *are used both for the georgeous yellow color they impart and for their disinctive flavor. Saffron from La Mancha, in Spain, is the nearest to that used in Morocco. The filaments need to be crushed or soaked in liquid before use so that their flavor is fully released during cooking. In Morocco, saffron is crushed with a little salt before being added to the pan.*

Sesame seeds (zenjlan) *The annual herb,* Sesamum indicum, *was one of the first oil-yielding plants to be cultivated in the Near East. The seeds are normally toasted before being used in breads or sweets, or to garnish tagines.*

Spices *Tiny dried anise seeds are mostly used in baking, to flavor breads or tiny cookies. Caraway seeds are the main flavoring of a soup (see page 18) that is served with steamed lamb's heads, one of the staples of Moroccan street food.*

Cinnamon is used both in stick and ground form. It gives a distinctive flavor to some sweet-spicy tagines and egg and vegetable dishes, as well as sweets. Ground cinnamon is also used as a garnish. Cumin is an important spice—and smell—in the Moroccan kitchen. The ground seeds are usually added to cooked dishes and to salads. Ground cumin is also mixed with salt and used as a condiment. Ground ginger is another essential spice in the Moroccan pantry, and paprika is used extensively in soups, salads, stews, and vegetables. Paprika is often added at the end of cooking so that it keeps its color.

Vermicelli (fdawesh) *In Italian, vermicelli means "small worms," which very aptly describes the very thin pasta most commonly used in Moroccan soups. Vermicelli is also steamed like couscous and served with pigeons or meat. If buying vermicelli rolled into balls, you will need to break these up to produce strands about 1 inch long.*

Ingredients illustrated on previous pages
Top row *(from left to right) almonds; prunes and dates; honeycomb; flat-leaf parsley, mint, and purslane; short-grain rice, fine and very fine couscous; sage, cilantro, and coriander seeds.*
Middle row *(from left to right) saffron; extra virgin olive oil; ground ginger, cloves, and ground cumin; ras el hanout; green tea; vermicelli.*
Bottom row *(from left to right) paprika and sesame seeds; cinnamon sticks; crushed chili peppers; olives; orange flower water and rose water; preserved lemons.*

The Moroccan kitchen

An old-fashioned, traditional Moroccan kitchen is a large, sparsely furnished room with a few cushions or folded carpets laid on the tiled floor for the cook and her helpers to sit on. Water is taken from a ceramic or marble fountain, and food is cooked on earthenware braziers (*kanün*). Typical utensils are copper or cast-iron pots and pans; a selection of different-sized *tagines slaoui*, the glazed earthenware dishes with a conical lid used to cook and serve tagines (the name of the dish derives from the utensil); large and small *coucoussières*, the special steamers used for preparing couscous; and a couple of lightly rounded metal sheets, called *tbsil dial warqa*, to make *warqa* (Moroccan pastry, similar to phyllo).

The women spend much of their day in the kitchen and their work is never carried out in silence. When they run out of gossip, they break into nostalgic songs. Added to the patter of the women is the noise of the children playing in the kitchen or in the adjoining courtyard. The atmosphere is warm and feminine. Men are not usually welcome in the kitchen—their place is in the living room where they receive guests and make mint tea for them.

Fresh ingredients are bought daily in the *souks* or from local markets or grocers, to supplement the dried foodstuffs that are kept on shelves in airtight containers or canvas bags. There is a strong tradition of preserving foods. Depending on the season, the women preserve lemons in salt and pack different types of olives in brine or oil. They dry spiced strips of beef and cook them in fat to make *khlai'*, which they then pack in large earthenware jars (*khabia*) to last the year. Butter is clarified to make *s'men*; the longer it is kept and the more rancid it becomes, the more highly prized it is. Breads and pastries are stored in colorful straw baskets with pointed lids (*tbiqa*); hot food is taken to table in similar copper receptacles.

The preparation of Moroccan food generally requires little time and few specialist utensils: sharp knives; a small and a large mortar and pestle, the former to grind spices and the latter to crush herbs or garlic; wooden, straw, and earthenware bowls of different shapes and sizes used for a multitude of tasks; and large round sieves (*ghorbal*) to grade couscous grains.

You are most likely to find traditional kitchens in old houses in the *medinas* and in the villages. In the *villes nouvelles* that now surround the *medinas*, the modern apartment blocks have kitchens that are little different from those found in northern Europe and North America. You will still see a few traditional utensils, such as *tagines slaoui, coucoussières,* and silver-plated teapots, but the earthenware storage jars have been mostly replaced by plastic buckets.

Making *briouats*

A very thin pastry called *warqa* is usually used for *briouats*, the savory snacks with a multitude of fillings. Phyllo pastry is a good alternative (keep it covered with a damp cloth to prevent it from drying out).

You can shape *briouats* in three different ways: triangles, rectangles, or fingers. First divide the filling into the number of pastries the recipe will make, to be sure you don't use too much or too little. If you are going to deep-fry them, keep them covered with plastic wrap; if baking, brush both sides of the shaped pastries with melted butter and place on a rack in a roasting pan. Triangles: Place a sheet of phyllo pastry on your work surface, brush it with melted butter, and fold it in half lengthwise. Brush again with melted butter. Place 1–2 tablespoons of filling at the bottom of the pastry strip, about ¼ inch from the edge. Taking a corner of the pastry strip, fold the phyllo over the filling to form a triangle. Brush with butter.

Continue folding in a triangular fashion until you reach the other end, brushing with butter after each fold. Stick the end with a little water. Rectangles: Place a sheet of phyllo on your work surface and brush it with melted butter. Spread 1–2 tablespoons of filling in the middle, about ¼ inch from the top edge and about 2 inches from each side. Fold one side in over the filling, then fold in the other (the two should not overlap). Brush with butter. Tuck in the top edge, then fold down into a rectangle about 3 by 2 inches. Stick the end with a little water. Fingers: Shape as for rectangles, but roll into fingers measuring 3–4 inches long.

Cooking tagines

Tagines are stews cooked in the dish of the same name or in a wide casserole (*tawa*). The best casseroles, or Dutch ovens, to use are cast-iron, copper, or aluminum ones. Those made from stainless steel can stick and do not conduct the heat as efficiently, and the cooking broth might not reduce in the time stated in the recipe. Tagines can be made with meat—most commonly lamb—as well as variety meats, poultry, game, or fish. The garnishes are fresh or dried vegetables or fruit, eggs, grains, nuts, or legumes.

There are four basic tagine sauces: *k'dra*, *m'qalli*, *m'hammer*, and *m'chermel* (see page 72) and can be varied by altering the herbs and spices. They can also be made sweet with a little honey or confectioners' sugar, or fragrant with orange flower water.

Tagines are traditionally simmered over low heat for 2–2½ hours or until the meat falls off the bone and the cooking liquid is reduced to a thick, unctuous sauce. To save time, I prefer to boil them quite hard, over medium-high heat with the pan covered. Check the sauce regularly and stir to see if it is sticking, in which case add a little water. If it is still too runny toward the end of the cooking time, raise the heat and boil uncovered until reduced. The resulting tagine will be just as good as one that has been cooked long and slow.

Below *Egg and Herb Triangles (page 31)*

SOUPS

AND APPETIZERS

Chick Pea and Lamb Soup

Harira

Harira seems to be every Moroccan's favorite late-afternoon snack. Moreover, it is what is first eaten when the fast during Ramadan is broken. Harira is normally served with a sweet accompaniment, such as dates or Tressed Pastries (page 116), but it is sometimes eaten with a savory dish such as potato cakes (see page 98). Harira can be varied in many different ways. You can use kefta *(see page 54) instead of diced lamb. The chick peas can be replaced with dried split fava beans or lentils, and the vermicelli with short-grain rice, rinsed before use, or* m'hamssa *(big couscous grains).* **Serves 4–6**

⅓ cup dried chick peas
soaked overnight with ½ teaspoon baking soda added to the water

½ pound boneless neck of lamb
cut into small cubes

1 large onion *thinly sliced*

1 bunch fresh flat-leaf parsley
most of bottom stems discarded, then minced (about ¾ cup)

pinch of saffron filaments *crushed*

¼ teaspoon ground ginger

sea salt and finely ground black pepper

1 x 16-ounce can Italian plum tomatoes *coarsely chopped*

4 tablespoons butter

2 ounces vermicelli *broken into ¾-inch pieces (about ½ cup)*

1 bunch cilantro *most of bottom stems discarded, then minced (about ¾ cup)*

1 tablespoon tomato paste

juice of 2 lemons, or to taste

3–4 tablespoons all-purpose flour

1 Drain and rinse the chick peas. Spread them on a clean cloth, cover them with another cloth, and, with a rolling pin, crush lightly to split them in half and loosen their skin. Put them in a bowl of water and stir with your hand. The skins should float to the surface, which will make them easy to remove and discard.

2 Put the drained chick peas into a large saucepan. Add the lamb, onion, parsley, spices, 1 teaspoon pepper, the tomatoes and their juice, and 3 quarts water. Bring to a boil. Drop in the butter, cover, and leave to boil over medium-high heat for 1 hour.

3 Stir in the vermicelli, cilantro, tomato paste, and lemon juice. Reduce the heat under the pan to low.

4 Mix the flour with 1 cup water. Dribble this mixture into the soup, stirring constantly to prevent lumps from forming. The soup should thicken to a velvety consistency. Add sea salt to taste and simmer for a few more minutes, or until the vermicelli is cooked. Check the seasoning, then serve very hot.

Mint and Caraway Soup

Harira Krawiya

This is a wonderfully refreshing soup that can be served hot or cold (although the latter is not traditional). It has a rather unusual taste and a slightly crunchy texture because of the caraway seeds. It is generally served with baked lambs' heads, which are a main feature of street breakfasts. The soup helps to counteract the rather rich meat of the heads. **Serves 4–6**

6 tablespoons all-purpose flour

¼ teaspoon mastic
crushed to a powder

4 or 5 sprigs of fresh mint
leaves only, minced

1½ tablespoons caraway seeds
coarsely ground

sea salt

juice of 1 lemon, or to taste

lemon wedges to serve

1 Bring 2 quarts of water to a boil in a large saucepan, then remove from the heat.

2 Meanwhile, mix the flour and powdered mastic with 1¼ cups cold water to produce a smooth, milky liquid. Pour this slowly into the hot water, stirring continuously so that it does not form lumps. Return to medium-high heat and bring back to a boil, still stirring.

3 Add the mint, ground caraway, and salt to taste. Lower the heat and simmer for 15 minutes, stirring regularly.

4 Stir in the lemon juice. Taste and adjust the seasoning if necessary. Serve hot or cold, with lemon wedges on the side.

Dried Fava Bean Soup

Beyssara

Beyssara, *or* Beyssar, *depending on who you speak to, is a street-breakfast staple, somewhere between a thick soup and a thin purée. In Marrakesh, it is cooked in large, round earthenware jars, which are balanced over charcoal fires in a tilted position. The narrow opening of the jar faces the cook and he ladles the soup out into bowls using a long-handled spoon.* **Serves 4–6**

1 Rinse the fava beans, which will have swelled to twice their original size, and put them in a large saucepan. Add the unpeeled garlic cloves and the spices and cover with water (about 2 quarts). Bring to a boil over medium-high heat, then cover the pan and leave to boil for 30 minutes or until the fava beans have turned into a mush.

2 Reduce the heat to low and simmer for a further 10–15 minutes.

3 Discard the garlic and add sea salt to taste. Pour into a shallow serving bowl, drizzle olive oil all over, and sprinkle with a little more cumin. Serve very hot, with more oil and cumin for those who like it.

2 cups dried split fava beans
soaked overnight with 1 teaspoon baking soda added to the water

2 unpeeled garlic cloves

1½ teaspoons each ground cumin and paprika

scant ½ teaspoon dried hot chili peppers crushed to a coarse powder, or to taste

sea salt

extra virgin olive oil

Carrot Salad with Chili and Cumin

Khizü Mrqed

I have never been a great aficionado of boiled carrots, always associating them with boring hospital food (not that I have spent any time in hospitals), but when I first tasted this salad in Morocco I changed my mind. The piquant dressing nicely counterbalances the sweetness of the carrots and gives the salad a rather delicate flavor. **Serves 4–6**

1 Put the carrot pieces and peeled garlic cloves into a saucepan and cover with water. Bring to a boil over a medium-high heat, then cover and leave to boil for 10 minutes or until the carrots are tender. Drain and leave to cool. Discard the garlic cloves.

2 Combine the remaining ingredients in a salad bowl and mix well together. Add the carrots. Toss carefully, then taste and adjust the seasoning if necessary. Serve at room temperature.

1¾ pounds carrots *quartered and then cut across in half, or into fine strips if using large carrots*

3 garlic cloves

½ teaspoon dried hot chili peppers crushed to a coarse powder, or to taste

1½ teaspoons each paprika and ground cumin

½ bunch each fresh flat-leaf parsley and cilantro *most of bottom stems discarded, then minced (about ⅓ cup each)*

1½ tablespoons white wine vinegar

⅓ cup extra virgin olive oil

sea salt to taste

Steamed Eggplant in a Tomato and Cilantro Sauce

Za'lüq

This delectable cooked salad has a soft but chunky texture. You can also serve it as a vegetarian main course, in which case double the quantities. For a different flavor, use parsley instead of the cilantro. **Serves 4–6**

1 pound eggplants

3 garlic cloves

6 tablespoons extra virgin olive oil

1 x 28-ounce can Italian peeled plum tomatoes *drained, seeded, and coarsely chopped*

2 bunches cilantro *most of bottom stems discarded, then minced (about 1½ cups)*

½ teaspoon ground cumin

juice of ½ lemon, or to taste

¼ teaspoon paprika

⅛ teaspoon dried hot chili peppers crushed to a coarse powder, or to taste

sea salt and finely ground black pepper

1 Peel the eggplants lengthwise, leaving thin strips of skin. Quarter them lengthwise and then slice across into pieces about ½ inch thick.

2 Steam the eggplant pieces and peeled garlic cloves for 30 minutes or until soft. (If you don't have a steamer, boil them for 15 minutes or until tender, then drain well.)

3 Meanwhile, pour the oil into a sauté pan, add the chopped tomatoes, cilantro, and cumin, and mix well together. Place over medium-high heat and cook for about 15 minutes, or until excess juices have evaporated and the sauce looks fresh and chunky. Stir occasionally during cooking.

4 When the eggplant and garlic are ready, mash them with a fork or a potato masher. Don't use a food processor, because the eggplant will become too mushy.

5 Add the mashed eggplant to the tomato sauce, along with the lemon juice, paprika, crushed chilies, salt to taste, and ⅛ teaspoon pepper. Mix well together and simmer over low heat for a further 15 minutes, stirring regularly.

6 Taste and adjust the seasoning if necessary, then leave to cool. Serve at room temperature.

Sweet Tomato Confit

Matecha M'assala

The Moroccans serve this dish, which is really more like a jam than a salad, as part of their salades variées. I sometimes serve it Italian-style, spooned onto good toasted bread to make sweet-spicy crostini. **Serves 4**

1 Put the tomatoes in a wide saucepan with the butter, onion, saffron, a little sea salt, and scant 1 teaspoon pepper. Place over medium heat, cover, and boil for 45–50 minutes, stirring regularly. The tomatoes should reduce and become very concentrated. If any excess liquid remains, boil uncovered for a further 5–10 minutes, stirring almost continuously.

2 Add the honey and cinnamon and cook, stirring, for a few more minutes. Leave to cool, then transfer to a serving platter and sprinkle with the toasted sesame seeds. Serve at room temperature.

3 x 28-ounce cans Italian plum tomatoes *drained, halved lengthwise, and seeded*

7 tablespoons butter

1 medium-sized onion *thinly sliced*

pinch of saffron filaments *crushed*

sea salt and finely ground black pepper

3 tablespoons honey

1 teaspoon ground cinnamon

2 tablespoons sesame seeds *toasted*

Grilled Pepper and Tomato Salad

Chakchūka

Moroccan sweet peppers are long, thin-fleshed, and slightly piquant in flavor. You can find the same type in Greek or Cypriot markets. If you are going to use this sort of pepper, increase the quantity to 6, as they are smaller than green bell peppers. You can turn this salad into a hot appetizer by adding eggs: When the tomatoes and peppers are nearly ready, break 4 eggs over them and cook for about 5 minutes or until the eggs are set to your liking. **Serves 4–6**

4 medium-sized green bell peppers

3 x 28-ounce cans Italian plum tomatoes *drained, seeded, and coarsely chopped*

6 tablespoons extra virgin olive oil

2 garlic cloves *minced*

scant ½ teaspoon dried hot chili peppers crushed to a coarse powder, or to taste

1 teaspoon paprika

sea salt

1 preserved lemon, peel only *cut lengthwise into strips* **(optional)**

1 bunch fresh flat-leaf parsley *most of bottom stems discarded, then minced (about ¾ cup)*

1 Grill the peppers over a charcoal fire, or cook under the broiler, for 10–15 minutes or until the skin is charred and blistered on all sides and the flesh has softened. Leave until cool enough to handle, then peel them and remove the seeds and core. Cut the flesh into small squares or strips.

2 Combine the tomatoes, olive oil, garlic, and chilies in a large frying pan. Add the paprika and salt to taste and cook over medium-high heat for 15–20 minutes, stirring occasionally, until the tomatoes have reduced and almost all excess liquid has evaporated.

3 Add the peppers, preserved lemon, and parsley to the tomato sauce. Cook, stirring occasionally, for a further 5–10 minutes, or until the sauce has become very concentrated. Remove from the heat and leave to cool. Serve at room temperature.

Preserved Lemons

Preserved lemons are easy to prepare at home. You will need 5–6 medium-sized unwaxed lemons (about 1½ pounds) for a 1-quart jar. Quarter the lemons lengthwise, keeping them attached at the stem end, then carefully prize them open and spread 1 teaspoon coarse sea salt inside each half. Pack the lemons tightly into the jar and place a well-scrubbed heavy stone (or other weight) on top to press them, so that they exude as much juice as possible. Seal the jar and leave to mature for 4 weeks before using.

Sweet Potato Salad with Cumin and Ginger

Batata Hleewa bel kammün wa skinjibir

In Shakespeare's day, sweet potatoes were candied and sold as an aphrodisiac, although in Morocco they are just seen as an exciting variation on the more common potato. The saffron gives pale-fleshed sweet potatoes a very pretty yellow color. For a delicious light vegetarian lunch, serve the potatoes with the bright orange Carrot Salad with Chili and Cumin (page 21) and the deep green Sautéed Purée of Herbs (page 96). All three salads can be made a day in advance as they keep well. **Serves 4–6**

6 tablespoons extra virgin olive oil

2 small onions *thinly sliced*

good pinch of saffron filaments *crushed*

¾ teaspoon ground ginger

1¾ pounds yellow-fleshed sweet potatoes *peeled, quartered, and cut into chunks*

¾ teaspoon ground cumin

1½ teaspoons paprika

juice of 1½ lemons, or to taste

sea salt

½ bunch each fresh flat-leaf parsley and cilantro *most of bottom stems discarded, then minced (about ⅓ cup each)*

1 Heat the olive oil in a saucepan over medium heat. Add the onions, crushed saffron, and ginger and sauté until the onions have a soft texture and are translucent.

2 Add the sweet potatoes, cumin, paprika, lemon juice, and sea salt to taste. Half cover with water (about 1 cup) and bring to a boil. Cover and let boil for 10–15 minutes or until the sweet potatoes are tender and the sauce has thickened.

3 Carefully stir in the minced herbs. Taste and adjust the seasoning if necessary, then remove from the heat. Move the lid a little so that the pan is not completely covered, and leave to cool. Serve warm or at room temperature.

Tomato and Onion Salad

Shlada Dial Matecha

In Morocco, this salad always accompanies grilled meat, variety meats, or fish. At some stalls they purée the tomatoes and grate the onions; on others they cut the tomatoes in wedges and slice the onions; and on others they chop both quite small. The latter is my favorite version. In the old port of Essaouira, I had this salad dressed with argan oil (see page 10), which gave it a subtle nutty taste. You can replace the onions with cucumber, which should be peeled and seeded before being diced like the tomatoes. **Serves 4–6**

1 Put the diced tomatoes, parsley, and onions in a salad bowl. Add the cumin, lemon juice, and oil. Season with salt to taste and 1 teaspoon pepper.

2 Toss well together. Taste and adjust the seasoning if necessary. Serve at room temperature.

2¼ pounds firm vine-ripened tomatoes *seeded and diced into small cubes*

1 bunch fresh flat-leaf parsley *most of bottom stems discarded, then minced (about ¾ cup)*

2 medium-sized red onions *minced*

1 teaspoon ground cumin

juice of 2 lemons, or to taste

5 tablespoons extra virgin olive oil or argan oil

sea salt and finely ground black pepper

Fava Bean Salad

Shlada del Fül

The cooking time for fava beans varies according to their size and age. Fresh fava beans will take only about 10 minutes to cook, or even less if they are very small (use only 1 cup water). Garden peas can be substituted, to make a dish with a sweeter taste. **Serves 4**

1 If using frozen beans, thaw by plunging them into boiling water and then draining. Put the beans into a saucepan and add the onion, oil, and sea salt to taste. Cover with water (about 1½ cups). Bring to a boil over medium-high heat, then cover and let boil for about 10 minutes.

2 Add the minced cilantro, paprika, and lemon juice and cook, covered, for a further 5 minutes, or until the fava beans are tender and the sauce has reduced.

3 Transfer to a serving dish, garnish with the strips of preserved lemon, and serve hot, warm, or at room temperature.

1 pound shelled fava beans, fresh or frozen

1 small onion *thinly sliced*

3 tablespoons extra virgin olive oil

sea salt

1 bunch cilantro *most of bottom stems discarded, then minced (about ¾ cup)*

1 teaspoon paprika

juice of ½ lemon, or to taste

To serve:

½ preserved lemon, peel only *cut lengthwise into thin strips*

Merguez Fingers

Briouat bel Merguez

Merguez *(the word* mirguaz *actually means sausage) are small, spicy lamb sausages heavily seasoned with paprika, garlic, fennel seeds, and pepper. They are popular throughout North Africa, and recently in Europe too—especially in Paris, where they are sold on the streets in baguettes with frites. Although not widely available in the U.S., they can usually be found in some ethnic or specialty food stores. The western version of the sausage is twice as long as that made in Morocco—6 inches instead of 3 inches. On the streets of Morocco, merguez are grilled or fried, but you can also wrap them in crisp phyllo pastry to make great finger food. Briouts are always deep-fried in Morocco, but I prefer to bake them—the taste is not quite authentic, but it is still delicious.* **Makes 16 fingers**

8 *merguez* sausages (each about 6 inches long) or 16 smaller ones

16 sheets of phyllo pastry (each about 13 by 7 inches)

2 tablespoons unsalted butter
melted

2 tablespoons vegetable oil for deep-frying (optional)

1 Sauté the sausages in a non-stick pan over medium-high heat for about 5 minutes or until they are lightly browned on all sides. Transfer to several layers of paper towel to drain well. Cut the sausages in half if they are large.

2 Make the fingers, following the instructions on pages 12–13. Deep-fry for 2–3 minutes on each side or until golden brown. Alternatively, bake in a preheated oven at 350°F for 20–25 minutes. Serve hot or warm.

Egg and Herb Triangles

Briouat bel Beyd

These are one of my favorite briouats—*easy and quick to make, with a wonderfully moist filling inside crunchy pastry. The trick here is to avoid overcooking the eggs, because they continue to cook inside the pastry. The scrambled egg filling, subtly flavored with saffron, is also good served on its own as a first course.* **Makes 16 triangles**

1 Put the olive oil and onions in a large frying pan and place over medium heat. Fry until soft and translucent, stirring occasionally. Add the herbs, spices, and ¼ teaspoon pepper. Reduce the heat to medium-low and fry for 5 more minutes.

2 Meanwhile, beat the eggs with sea salt to taste. When the onions are completely soft, add the eggs and scramble for 7–10 minutes, or until just set. Don't leave them too runny or they will make the pastry soggy. Taste and adjust the seasoning if necessary, then leave to cool.

3 Make the triangles, or rectangles if you prefer, following the instructions on pages 12–13, using 1½ tablespoons filling per pastry. Deep-fry for 2–3 minutes on each side or until golden brown. Alternatively, bake in a preheated oven at 350°F for 20–25 minutes. Serve hot or warm.

¼ cup extra virgin olive oil

3 medium-sized onions *minced*

1 bunch each cilantro and fresh flat-leaf parsley *most of bottom stems discarded, then minced (about ¾ cup each)*

pinch of saffron filaments *crushed*

½ teaspoon ground cinnamon

sea salt and finely ground black pepper

8 free-range eggs

16 sheets of phyllo pastry (each about 13 by 7 inches)

vegetable oil for deep-frying (optional)

Quail and Almond Triangles

Briouat el-Bstila

The luscious filling used in these briouats *is the same as that used for* Pastilla, *one of the great dishes of Moroccan cuisine. While* Pastilla *is not a dish for informal eating, you do find* briouats *on the streets. Traditionally the filling is made with pigeons, which in Morocco are quite gamy; quails are a good substitute.* **Makes 16 triangles**

3 quails

1 medium-sized onion *minced*

a few sprigs each of fresh flat-leaf parsley and cilantro *most of bottom stems discarded, then minced*

¾ teaspoon each ground cinnamon and ground ginger

½ teaspoon ground *ras el hanout*

⅛ teaspoon dried hot chili peppers crushed to a coarse powder, or to taste

pinch of saffron filaments *crushed*

sea salt

6 tablespoons unsalted butter

⅓ cup blanched almonds

5 free-range eggs *lightly beaten*

1 tablespoon confectioners' sugar

16 sheets of phyllo pastry (each about 13 by 7 inches)

vegetable oil for deep-frying

To serve:

confectioners' sugar and ground cinnamon

1 Put the quails in a saucepan. Add the onion, herbs, ¼ teaspoon of the cinnamon, the remaining spices, and a little salt. Pour in 2 cups water and bring to a boil over medium-high heat. Add 4 tablespoons of the butter and stir until melted, then cover and boil for 20 minutes. Turn the heat down to medium-low, and turn the birds in the sauce. Simmer, covered, for a further 10 minutes or until the birds are tender.

2 Meanwhile, sauté the almonds in the remaining 2 tablespoons butter until golden brown. Leave to cool, then grind coarsely in a food processor.

3 Transfer the quails to a plate and leave to cool. The sauce should be very thick; if necessary, boil to reduce it, stirring occasionally. Turn the heat to low, then add the eggs to the sauce and stir for about 5 minutes or until they are scrambled. (Don't leave them runny or they will make the pastry soggy.) Remove from the heat.

4 Take the quail meat off the bone, discarding the skin, and tear into small pieces. Add to the egg mixture, along with the ground almonds, sugar, and remaining ½ teaspoon cinnamon. Mix well together. Season to taste.

5 Make the triangles following the instructions on pages 12–13, using 1½–2 tablespoons of filling per triangle. Deep-fry in hot vegetable oil for 2–3 minutes on each side or until golden brown. Sprinkle with confectioners' sugar and cinnamon, and serve hot.

Semolina Galettes

Harcha

You are almost always offered harcha *in the homes of peasants in the* rif *(countryside)— within minutes of your arrival, they will have mixed the dough, cooked it in an earthenware pan over a charcoal fire, and served it, accompanied by their own homemade butter and mint tea. Freshly prepared like this,* harcha *is simply delicious, but when eaten as a street snack it is sometimes disappointingly hard and tasteless. This recipe was given to me by a friend's cook in Rabat, who is an excellent baker. She shapes the semolina mixture into small round disks and serves them as party tidbits.* **Makes 30–35 small galettes**

1 cup + 2 tablespoons fine semolina flour

⅓ cup regular semolina

¼ teaspoon sea salt

2 tablespoons sugar

4 tablespoons butter *softened* **plus extra for frying**

To serve:

butter or honey

1 Put the semolina (fine and regular), salt, and sugar in a mixing bowl. Using your fingertips, work in the softened butter, then gradually add about ¼ cup water to bind to a firm dough. Knead it just enough to make it homogenous.

2 Roll out the dough to about ½-inch thickness. Using a 2-inch round biscuit cutter, or a glass with sharp edges, cut into disks (make them larger if you prefer). Gather up the trimmings and roll out again until all the dough has been used. Put the disks on a buttered plate.

3 Brush a large non-stick frying pan with softened butter and place over medium heat. When the pan is hot, add as many semolina disks as will fit comfortably. Cook for 1–2 minutes on each side. You don't want them to color much, just to become firm. Remove to a serving platter and serve hot, plain or with a dollop of butter or honey on each galette. You can also serve *harcha* warm or at room temperature.

Moroccan Bread

Ksra

The old tradition of baking bread in communal ovens is still very much alive in the souks *of Fez. Every day, at about lunchtime, young girls and boys stream past, carrying wooden trays on their heads, or in their arms, on which are two or more loaves on their way to the local oven—every* souk *has its own oven, bath, drinking fountain, mosque, and* medressa *(Koranic school). The recipe below comes from a small café in Casablanca, where the bread is particularly delicious. I cannot achieve the fluffy texture of the original, but I suspect it is because domestic ovens are never as hot as wood-fired ones.* **Makes 1 medium-sized loaf**

1 Put the flour into a shallow mixing bowl. Add the yeast, salt, anise seed, and sesame seeds. Gradually pour in 1 cup tepid water, mixing with your hands. Knead energetically for about 10 minutes or until you have a firm, elastic dough.

2 Roll the dough into a ball and flatten it with your floured hand until you have a round about 8 inches wide and ¾ in thick. Place on a floured baking sheet and cover with a clean cloth. Leave to rise in a warm place for about 1½ hours.

3 Bake in a preheated oven at 400°F for 45–50 minutes or until the bread sounds hollow when tapped on the base.

4 Leave the bread to cool slightly on a rack, then serve warm (when the bread is at its best), or leave to cool completely. This bread, like all others, will freeze very well, but don't refrigerate it as the texture will change and it won't be good to eat.

3 cups whole-wheat flour

1 x ¼-ounce envelope rapid-rise dry yeast

1 teaspoon each sea salt and anise seed

1½ teaspoons sesame seeds *toasted*

Onion and Parsley Flat Breads

Rghäyef bel Besla wal Ma'danüs

You find these flat breads everywhere in the streets, where they are often rather chewy with hardly any taste. By contrast, r'ghäyef *made at home are quite delicious, with a lovely flaky texture. This comes from the same friend who gave me her recipe for* harcha.

Makes 12–14 mini flat breads

1 Put the flour into a mixing bowl and stir in the salt and yeast. Gradually add up to about ½ cup tepid water, working it with your fingers, until the dough has a loose consistency, slightly softer than that of bread dough. Knead until completely smooth and pliable: 15–20 minutes by hand or 5 minutes in a food processor, using the dough blade.

2 Put all the filling ingredients in a mixing bowl, add sea salt to taste, and mix well together.

3 Grease a large baking sheet with a little butter, then smear your working surface, rolling pin, and hands with butter. Pinch off half of the dough and roll it out very thinly (¹⁄₁₆ inch). Cut into 5-inch squares. Spread 1 tablespoon of filling over one half of each square; fold the other side over and then fold again to form a square measuring about 2½ inches across. Flatten the square with your hand and place on the greased baking sheet. Continue filling and shaping breads until you have finished both dough and filling, not forgetting to use the cut-out pieces of dough (if you have any dough left over, form it into squares and bake it plain). Keep buttering your hands, working surface, and rolling pin to prevent sticking.

4 Bake in a preheated oven at 375°F for 10 minutes, then turn the breads over and bake for a further 5 minutes or until they are golden and slightly crisp. Serve hot or warm.

For the dough:

1 cup all-purpose plain flour

¾ teaspoon each sea salt and rapid-rise dry yeast

For the filling:

1 medium-sized onion
minced

1 bunch fresh flat-leaf parsley
most of bottom stems discarded, then minced (about ¾ cup)

3 tablespoons unsalted butter
softened **plus extra for greasing**

½ teaspoon ground cumin

1 teaspoon paprika

⅛ teaspoon dried hot chili peppers crushed to a coarse powder, or to taste

sea salt

Rice Rectangles

Briouat bel rozz

These may seem a rather unusual appetizer or snack, but sweet-spicy flavors are one of the distinctive features of Moroccan cooking. The filling of sweetened rice has a soft, milky texture, which comes as a surprise after the crunchy bite of the crisp pastry. Some cooks add crushed toasted almonds to the rice. **Makes 16 rectangles**

1 cup milk

9 tablespoons short-grain rice *rinsed thoroughly*

4 tablespoons butter

sea salt

2 tablespoons confectioners' sugar

1 tablespoon orange flower water

16 sheets of phyllo pastry (each about 13 by 7 inches)

vegetable oil for deep-frying (optional)

To serve:

confectioners' sugar and ground cinnamon

1 Put the milk and ½ cup water in a saucepan and bring to a boil. Add the rice, butter, and a little sea salt and stir. Lower the heat, cover, and simmer for 10 minutes, stirring regularly.

2 Add the confectioners' sugar and orange flower water and cook, uncovered, for 5 minutes, stirring constantly. The rice should be slightly *al dente*, as it will continue to cook in the pastry. Cover with a clean cloth and leave to cool, stirring from time to time.

3 Make the rectangles, or other shapes, following the instructions on pages 12–13, using 1½ tablespoons filling per rectangle. Deep-fry in hot vegetable oil for 2–3 minutes on each side or until golden brown. Or, bake in a preheated oven at 350°F for 20–25 minutes. Serve hot, sprinkled with a little confectioners' sugar and ground cinnamon.

Moroccan Doughnuts

Sfinge

Sfinge-makers—usually men—are dotted all over the medina. In the not-so-distant past, you always found them next to the bakers of lambs' heads, because once it was the custom to eat sfinge with lambs' heads for breakfast. The sfinge-makers' dexterity and speed at handling such soft dough is quite astonishing. I always stop to watch them, hoping that one day I will learn to match their skills. **Makes 10–12 doughnuts**

1 Sift the flour into a bowl and stir in the salt and yeast. Gradually add up to 1 cup tepid water, mixing and kneading until you have a soft, sticky, and stretchy dough. Cover with a clean cloth and leave to rest in a warm place for 2–3 hours, until the dough is 3 or 4 times its original bulk.

2 When the dough is ready, pour enough vegetable oil to deep-fry the doughnuts into a large, deep frying pan and place over high heat.

3 Meanwhile, knead the dough again, until smooth and even in texture. Smear your hands with a little cool vegetable oil, then pinch off a ball of dough, the size of a clementine. With your thumb, punch a hole through the middle. Stretch the dough to form a floppy bracelet and slide it into the hot oil, which should bubble around it.

4 Insert the handle of a metal spoon in the middle of the doughnut and stir it in the oil as if you are trying to make the opening wider (this is really to stop the middle from narrowing). Make and fry as many doughnuts as the pan will take comfortably. Fry for 2–4 minutes on each side, turning them over several times to stop them from splitting, until golden brown all over. Drain on several layers of paper towel. (The *sfinge*-makers have a large white enamel dish with a raised center on which they balance the doughnuts to drain off the oil.) Serve hot or at room temperature, either plain or with honey or sugar.

2 cups all-purpose flour

1 teaspoon sea salt

2 teaspoons rapid-rise dry yeast

vegetable oil for deep-frying

To serve:

honey or granulated sugar

MAIN
DISHES

Swordfish Brochettes

Qotbane del Hüt

Fish for brochettes, like meat, is traditionally cut quite small, but you can cut it to the size you prefer (increase the cooking time accordingly). You can replace the swordfish with monkfish, tuna, or any other dense-fleshed fish. These brochettes make a delicious quick summer lunch and are particularly tasty if grilled over a charcoal fire. **Serves 4–6**

1¾ pounds swordfish
cut into 1-inch cubes

1 bunch fresh flat-leaf parsley
most of bottom stems discarded, then minced (about ¾ cup)

2 garlic cloves *minced*

¼ teaspoon dried hot chili peppers crushed to a coarse powder, or to taste

2 teaspoons each ground cumin and paprika

sea salt

1 Put the cubes of swordfish in a mixing bowl. Add the parsley, garlic, spices, and salt to taste and mix well together. Leave to marinate for at least 2 hours.

2 Thread the fish cubes onto 8 or 12 long skewers (2 skewers per person). Grill over a charcoal fire, or cook under a preheated broiler (as near the heat as you can), for 2–3 minutes on each side or until the fish is done to your liking. Don't cook it too long or it will become rubbery. Serve immediately with Tomato and Onion Salad (page 27).

Fried Fish with Spicy Cilantro Sauce
Hüt bel Chermüla

Fried fish is one of the staples of Moroccan street food, both in coastal towns and inland, except that away from the sea you will only find it on certain days. The fish most commonly fried is sardines. These are boned and butterflied (a time-consuming task) and a little chermüla is spread on the inside before pairs of fish are put together, dipped into flour, and fried. Pieces of filleted fish such as flounder are an easy alternative. **Serves 4–6**

For the *chermüla*:

5 garlic cloves *minced*

1 small onion *thinly sliced*

2 bunches cilantro *most of bottom stems discarded, then minced (about 1½ cups)*

1 teaspoon ground cumin

½ teaspoon paprika

¼ teaspoon dried hot chili peppers crushed to a coarse powder, or to taste

6 tablespoons extra virgin olive oil

juice of 2 lemons, or to taste

sea salt

For the fish:

2¼ pounds white flounder fillets *cut into manageable pieces*

all-purpose flour for coating

vegetable oil for deep-frying

1 Combine all the ingredients for the *chermüla* in a bowl, adding salt to taste. Mix well together. Add the fish and leave to marinate for at least 2 hours or overnight in the refrigerator.

2 Remove the fish from the marinade, drain well, and dip into flour to coat all over. Set aside.

3 Pour enough vegetable oil to deep-fry the fish into a large frying pan and place over high heat. When the oil is very hot, slip in the fish pieces and fry, in batches, for 1–2 minutes on each side or until golden. Be careful not to overcook the fish or it will lose its delicate texture. Remove with a slotted spoon to several layers of paper towel to drain. Serve hot, warm, or at room temperature. Fava Bean Salad (page 29) is a good accompaniment.

Gray Mullet Stuffed with Swiss Chard

Hüt M'ammar bel Silq

Stuffing fish is very common in Morocco, and many different fillings are used, ranging from rice and olives or mashed potatoes (see Potato Cakes with Cilantro on page 98) to the Swiss chard and olive mixture below. **Serves 4–6**

1 Rub the *chermüla* all over the fish, inside and out, and leave to marinate for at least 2 hours in a cool place.

2 Meanwhile, put the Swiss chard and olives in the top of a steamer. Cover and steam over high heat for 15–20 minutes or until the chard is *al dente*. Remove from the heat and lift off the top part of the steamer. Take off the lid, cover with a cloth, and leave the chard to cool. (There is no need to season the chard, as the fish marinade will eventually flavor it.)

3 Spread the parsley sprigs over the bottom of a baking dish large enough to take all the fish. Fill each fish with as much of the Swiss chard and olive mixture as it will take, not forgetting the head cavity, and lay on the bed of parsley. Pour the remaining *chermüla* all over the fish. Bake in a preheated oven at 425°F, allowing 20–25 minutes for 4 small fish or 25–30 minutes for 2 larger ones.

4 If there is any Swiss chard left over, heat it gently with about 1 tablespoon extra virgin olive oil and serve alongside the fish.

chermüla (see Fried Fish with Spicy Cilantro Sauce, opposite)

4 gray mullets (about 1 pound each) or 2 gray mullets (2 pounds each) *cleaned*

1¾ pounds Swiss chard leaves and stems *shredded into ½-inch strips*

1¼ cups purple or black olives *pitted and cut in half*

a few sprigs of fresh flat-leaf parsley

Baked Sea Bass with Tomatoes and Olives

Dar'i bel Zeytün Mslalla

You can prepare this dish with most salt- or fresh-water fish as long as the flesh is firm and white. Make sure your fish is at room temperature before you bake it so that it cooks perfectly. Also, use good, flavorful tomatoes as they are the main accompaniment. **Serves 4**

1 Pat the fish dry and rub inside and out with the *chermüla*. Leave to marinate for 2 hours at room temperature, or longer in the refrigerator.

2 Spread the parsley sprigs over the bottom of an oven-to-table baking dish large enough to hold the 2 fish (or use 2 dishes, if necessary). Lay the fish in the dish and cover with the sliced tomatoes. Sprinkle with sea salt to taste and pour the *chermüla* all over. Bake in a preheated oven at 425°F for 25 minutes.

3 About 15 minutes before the fish is ready, soak the green olives in boiling water for 5 minutes. Drain well and arrange them over the fish. Finish baking, then serve hot.

2 whole sea bass (1¾ pounds each) *scaled, cleaned, and rinsed*

***chermüla* (see Fried Fish with Spicy Cilantro Sauce, page 46)**

a few sprigs of fresh flat-leaf parsley

1¾ pounds firm, vine-ripened tomatoes *cut into medium-thick slices*

sea salt

2 cups pitted green olives

49

Conger Eel with Onions and Raisins

Sannür bel Besla wa Zbib

This dish is a specialty of Essaouira, a lovely old port town in the south, where Orson Welles filmed Othello. *You can bake the eel on a bed of sliced carrots, as below, or on a bed of parsley sprigs. Another fish that goes well with this garnish is rainbow trout. Choose 4 trout weighing up to 14 ounces each. They will take less time to cook, about 20–25 minutes.*
Serves 4–6

7 tablespoons unsalted butter

6 medium-sized onions *thinly sliced*

1⅓ cups golden raisins

2 teaspoons each ground ginger and cinnamon

¼ teaspoon grated nutmeg

sea salt

1 pound carrots
sliced into thin rounds

2¼ pounds conger eel
cut into 6 steaks

¼ cup extra virgin olive oil

1 Put the butter, onions, raisins, half of the ginger and cinnamon, the nutmeg, and a little sea salt in a large frying pan. Place over medium heat and stir until the butter has melted. Continue to cook, stirring occasionally, until the onions are soft and translucent. Taste and adjust the seasoning if necessary, and set aside.

2 Spread the carrot slices over the bottom of an oven-to-table baking dish large enough to take the pieces of fish comfortably. Mix 1 teaspoon salt with the remaining ginger and cinnamon in a saucer. Rub the fish with the spice mixture, then lay on top of the carrots. Cover with the onion and raisin mixture and pour in the oil. Use ¼ cup water to deglaze the pan in which you cooked the onions, and pour the liquid over the fish.

3 Bake in a preheated oven at 350°F for 35–40 minutes or until the fish is tender and the onions slightly caramelized. Serve very hot.

10/27/1, SAT

Mussels with Tomatoes and Cilantro
Büzrüq

Büzrüq *is common in seaside towns and ports, and this recipe was given to me by a charming café owner in the* kasbah *of Oudaia in Rabat. The* kasbah *overlooks the sea and is on the original site of the city. You reach it through a superb twelfth-century gate. Just below the residential quarter is a perfect Andalusian garden, teeming with young students, sitting under trees and studying, away from their large, noisy families.* **Serves 4–6**

1 Pour the olive oil into a Dutch oven. Add the tomatoes with their juice, 1¼ cups water, the minced cilantro, garlic, salt to taste, and 1 teaspoon black pepper. Bring to a boil over medium-high heat, then cover the pan and leave to boil for 35–45 minutes or until the tomato sauce has thickened.

2 When the sauce is ready, stir in the mussels. Put the lid back on the pot and cook for 2–3 minutes or until the mussels have opened (discard any that remain closed). Don't overcook the mussels, or they will become rubbery and tasteless.

3 Taste the sauce and adjust the seasoning if necessary. Serve hot or cold.

¼ cup extra virgin olive oil

1 x 28-ounce can Italian plum tomatoes *coarsely chopped*

2 bunches cilantro *most of bottom stems discarded, then minced (about 1½ cups)*

3 garlic cloves *minced*

sea salt and finely ground black pepper

2¼ pounds large mussels *scrubbed and beards removed (discard any that do not close when tapped sharply)*

Eggs with Prawns and Cilantro

Tajen Ftooma

This frittata-like dish has a delicate lemony taste. The recipe comes from a man in Tetouan, who has a delightful little restaurant not far from the superb fish market there. Have the prawns ready to use at room temperature to make sure they will heat up thoroughly in the time it takes for the eggs to cook. **Serves 4**

6 tablespoons extra virgin olive oil

6 garlic cloves *minced*

5 bunches cilantro
most of bottom stems discarded, then minced (about 3¾ cups)

¾ teaspoon ground cumin

sea salt

juice of 1 lemon, or to taste

9 free-range eggs

¼ teaspoon dried hot chili peppers crushed to a coarse powder, or to taste

1¼ pounds peeled cooked tiger prawns or large shrimp

1 Heat the olive oil in a large sauté pan (preferably one from which you can serve at table). When the oil is hot, add the chopped garlic and cilantro and sauté for 1–2 minutes.

2 Add the cumin, 1½ cups water, and salt to taste and stir to mix. Bring to a boil over medium-high heat, then cover and leave to boil for 20–25 minutes, stirring occasionally, or until the sauce has reduced and there is hardly any water left. If necessary, boil uncovered until excess water has evaporated. Add the lemon juice and leave to bubble for a further 2–3 minutes.

3 Meanwhile, beat the eggs and season them with the crushed chilies and salt to taste.

4 Reduce the heat under the pan to low. Add the prawns to the sauce, stir, and spread them out evenly. Taste the sauce and adjust the seasoning if necessary, then add the eggs. Cover the pan and cook for 3–4 minutes or until the eggs are set to your liking. (I like to scramble the eggs rather than letting them set like a flat omelet.) Serve immediately.

Lamb Meatballs

Qotbane del Kefta

The best kefta *I have eaten were in Tangiers. There I had a charming guide, Rashid, who was born and brought up in the* medina, *and knew every single café, restaurant, and stall—and, of course, which ones were the best. He took me on a marvelous gastronomic tour of all these tiny places, culminating in a visit to a very old man who made the most exquisite* kefta. *The recipe below is his.* **Makes 24 brochettes**

1 medium-sized onion *quartered*

1 bunch each fresh flat-leaf parsley and cilantro
most of bottom stems discarded

2–3 sprigs of fresh mint, leaves only

2¼ pounds boneless lamb, preferably from the shoulder
ground

1 teaspoon each ground cumin and paprika

½ teaspoon each ground allspice, *ras el hanout* (optional), and hot dried chili peppers crushed to a coarse powder

sea salt

1 Put the onion, cilantro, parsley, and mint in a food processor and process until minced.

2 Put the ground lamb in a mixing bowl and add the minced onion and herbs, all the spices, and sea salt to taste. Mix with your hands until evenly combined. If you have a blender, process the meat mixture in it, in batches, for a very short time to make it a little smoother.

3 Divide the meat into 24 equal portions. Roll each portion into a ball and wrap it tightly around a skewer, squeezing it up and down, to form a sausage 4–6 inches long. Pinch it quite thin at each end.

4 Cook the *kefta* over a charcoal fire, or under a preheated broiler, for 3–4 minutes on each side or until they are done to your liking. Serve immediately. Fried Eggplants (page 97) and Tomato and Onion Salad (page 27) make good accompaniments.

Meatballs and Eggs in Tomato Sauce

Kefta bil Matecha wal Beyd

This is one of Morocco's most common tagines and one which visitors are likely to come across often. Traditionally the meatballs are parboiled for a few minutes before being added to the tomatoes, but as they cook very quickly I find that there is no need for the two separate steps. You can leave the eggs out altogether, if you prefer. **Serves 4–6**

1 Make the meat mixture as described in the Lamb Meatballs recipe, but stop after step 2. Cover with a clean cloth and set aside.

2 Put the olive oil, onions, and garlic in a large sauté pan (preferably one from which you can serve at table) and fry until the onions are soft and translucent. Pour in the chopped tomatoes and 1 cup water, and add the parsley, chilies, paprika, and salt to taste. Bring to a boil over medium-high heat, stirring occasionally, then remove from the heat.

3 Form the meat mixture into small balls the size of a quail egg (or large marble), moistening your hands with lightly salted water from time to time to prevent the meatballs from sticking. Drop the meatballs into the tomato sauce. Return the pan to the heat and leave to boil, covered, for 35–40 minutes or until the sauce has thickened. If necessary, remove the lid and boil uncovered until reduced.

4 Taste and adjust the seasoning if necessary. Make 4 spaces and break in the eggs. Cook for about 5 minutes or until the eggs are set to your liking. Serve immediately.

ingredients for Lamb Meatballs (see opposite)

4 free-range eggs

For the tomato sauce:

5 tablespoons extra virgin olive oil

2 medium-sized onions *thinly sliced*

2 garlic cloves *minced*

3 x 28-ounce cans Italian plum tomatoes *drained, seeded, and coarsely chopped*

1 bunch fresh flat-leaf parsley *most of bottom stems discarded, then minced (about ¾ cup)*

¼ teaspoon dried hot chili peppers crushed to a coarse powder, or to taste

1 teaspoon paprika

sea salt

Grilled Lamb's Liver

Küwa

If you want to have these brochettes on the streets of Morocco, you will be best off buying your liver from a butcher—where you should ask for a piece of caul fat as well—and then taking it to a grill house. There they will alternate the cubes of liver on the skewers with pieces of caul. Sometimes the liver is half-grilled, cut up into small pieces, and then caul is wrapped around each piece before the grilling is completed, in which case the dish is called bülfaf. *It is important to use very fresh, good quality liver for this dish; Moroccans use lamb's liver, but calf's liver can be substituted if you prefer.* **Serves 4–6**

1 Put the cubes of liver in a mixing bowl. Add the rest of the ingredients and mix well together. Leave to marinate for about 30 minutes at room temperature, or longer in the refrigerator.

2 Thread the liver onto 8–12 long skewers (allowing 2 skewers per person). Grill over a charcoal fire, or cook under a preheated broiler, for 1–2 minutes on each side or until the liver is cooked to your liking. Serve hot with wedges of lemon. Fava Bean Salad (page 29) and Tomato and Onion Salad (page 27) are good accompaniments.

1¾ pounds lamb's liver
diced into ¾-inch cubes

3 garlic cloves *minced*

1 bunch fresh flat-leaf parsley
*most of bottom stems discarded,
then minced (about ¾ cup)*

1 teaspoon each ground cumin and paprika

sea salt to taste

To serve:

lemon wedges

Tagine of Lamb with Fava Beans

Tajen Lham bel Fül

Vegetables and fruit grow large and luscious in Morocco. The most exciting places to buy them are the open-air markets, where you wade through mounds of seasonal produce, much of it picked that morning, and choose your own. I enjoy haggling with the merchants, as their prices almost always rise for foreigners. One gets a consolation prize for being overcharged, though, by being offered mint tea. When I was last there, fava beans were in season and the huge fleshy pods I got made those I buy in London seem very puny indeed.

Serves 4–6

2¼ pounds boneless neck or leg of lamb *cut into big chunks*

2 medium-sized onions *thinly sliced*

2 garlic cloves *minced*

5 tablespoons extra virgin olive oil

pinch of saffron filaments *crushed*

1 teaspoon ground ginger

sea salt and finely ground black pepper

1¾ pounds shelled fava beans, fresh or frozen

1½ bunches cilantro *most of bottom stems discarded, then minced (about 1¼ cups)*

juice of 1 lemon, or to taste

To serve:

½ preserved lemon, peel only *cut lengthwise into strips* **(optional)**

1 Put the lamb, onions, garlic, olive oil, spices, a little sea salt, and ½ teaspoon pepper in a Dutch oven. Cover with water (about 1 quart). Bring to a boil over medium-high heat, then cover and let boil for 30 minutes.

2 Meanwhile, if using frozen fava beans, thaw them by plunging into boiling water and then draining.

3 Turn the lamb in the sauce, then add the fava beans and cilantro. Cook, covered, for a further 25–30 minutes, stirring from time to time. If the sauce gets too thick, add a little water; if it is too runny, increase the heat to high and boil uncovered until reduced.

4 Stir in the lemon juice and simmer for a few more minutes. Taste and adjust the seasoning if necessary, then transfer to a serving dish. Garnish with the preserved lemon peel, if you are using it, and serve very hot.

Tagine of Lamb with Potatoes and Peas

Tajen Lham bel Btata wa Jeblana

This is one of the most common street tagines. The recipe here comes from a charming cook in the daily souk of Ourika. His tagines are all for 4 people or more, so in order to taste his food I had to buy a large one. Luckily I was sitting next to an army officer and his adorable daughter, who seemed to prefer my food to hers judging by the way she kept eyeing it. As I could never have finished my tagine on my own, I offered to share it with them. We had a jolly time tasting each other's dishes, and it was not long before they asked me to go with them to visit the grandmother, to taste her food, too. **Serves 4–6**

1 Put the lamb, onions, garlic, oil, spices, salt to taste, and ½ teaspoon pepper in a large Dutch oven. Barely cover with water (about 1 quart). Bring to a boil over medium-high heat, then cover and leave to boil for 50 minutes. After 30 minutes, turn the chunks of lamb in the sauce regularly.

2 Meanwhile, if using frozen peas, thaw them by plunging them into boiling water and draining.

3 Stir the herbs into the sauce, then add the potatoes and peas. Cook, covered, for a further 15 minutes, stirring occasionally, until both the vegetables and meat are done.

4 Taste and adjust the seasoning, if necessary. If the sauce is too runny, increase the heat to high and boil uncovered until reduced. Transfer the meat and vegetables to a serving dish and serve very hot.

2¼ pounds boneless neck or leg of lamb *cut into big chunks*

2 medium-sized onions *thinly sliced*

2 garlic cloves *minced*

¼ cup extra virgin olive oil

pinch of saffron filaments *crushed*

½ teaspoon each ground cumin and ginger

1 teaspoon paprika

sea salt and finely ground black pepper

2 cups shelled peas, fresh or frozen

1 bunch each fresh flat-leaf parsley and cilantro *most of bottom stems discarded, then minced (about ¾ cup each)*

1 pound potatoes *peeled and diced into bite-sized cubes*

Tagine of Chicken with Sweet Potatoes
Tajen Djaj bel Btata Lehleewa

The first time I ate this sweet-spicy tagine, in Aytourir, a daily souk *near Marrakesh, was a memorable experience. The tagine was to be cooked specially for me, so I had to gather the ingredients, and the chicken I bought was still alive. When I asked what I was to do with it, I was told to take it across to the stall where they kill, pluck, and clean the chickens. I watched as my poor, but luckily dead, chicken was held against a bizarre rotating machine to be plucked in seconds. On the way back to the stall, I bought sweet potatoes and golden raisins. A couple of hours later, I came back to find that my cook had excelled himself. Here is his delectable recipe.* **Serves 4**

1 Put the chicken, onion, and spices in a large Dutch oven. Add a little sea salt, ¾ teaspoon pepper, and the oil and half cover with water (about 1 quart). Bring to a boil over medium-high heat, then cover and leave to boil for 45–50 minutes or until the chicken is tender and the sauce has reduced by three-quarters.

2 Remove the chicken to a serving platter and keep warm. Add the sweet potatoes and raisins to the sauce. Lower the heat and simmer, covered, for 10 minutes or until the potatoes are tender and the raisins swollen. If the sauce is too runny, increase the heat to high and boil uncovered until reduced. Carefully stir in the honey, making sure you don't mash up the potatoes. Leave to bubble, uncovered, for a few more minutes. Taste and adjust the seasoning if necessary.

3 Arrange the sweet potatoes and raisins around the chicken and pour the sauce all over. Serve very hot.

1 free-range chicken (about 3¼ pounds)

1 medium-sized onion *thinly sliced*

pinch of saffron filaments *crushed*

½ teaspoon *ras el hanout*

1 teaspoon ground ginger

sea salt and finely ground black pepper

2 tablespoons extra virgin olive oil

1¾ pounds orange-fleshed sweet potatoes *peeled and cut into medium-sized chunks*

1⅓ cups golden raisins

3 tablespoons good honey

Chicken with Eggs

Djaj Souiri

This tagine is quite different from the traditional ones in that it looks more like a flat Spanish omelet than a stew. It has a distinct taste of cinnamon. Like most other tagines it can be prepared well in advance, but wait to add the eggs after reheating the chicken for serving. **Serves 4**

1 free-range chicken (about 3¼ pounds) *cut into 8 pieces*

1 medium-sized onion *thinly sliced*

2 tablespoons extra virgin olive oil

pinch of saffron filaments *crushed*

1 cinnamon stick

sea salt and finely ground black pepper

6 free-range eggs

½ teaspoon ground cinnamon

¼ teaspoon ground cumin

1 bunch fresh flat-leaf parsley *most of bottom stems discarded, then minced (about ¾ cup)*

juice of 1 lemon, or to taste

1 teaspoon paprika

1 Put the chicken pieces in a large, deep sauté pan that will just hold them snugly, and from which you can serve at table. Add the onion, olive oil, saffron, cinnamon stick, a little salt, and ½ teaspoon pepper. Cover with water (about 3½ cups). Bring to a boil over medium-high heat, then cover and let boil for 45 minutes or until the chicken is cooked and the sauce has thickened.

2 Meanwhile, lightly beat the eggs with the ground cinnamon, cumin, salt to taste, and ½ teaspoon pepper. Cover and set aside.

3 When the chicken is ready, remove the skin if you like. Stir the parsley and lemon juice into the sauce and leave to bubble for a few more minutes. If the sauce is too liquid, reduce it further by increasing the heat to high and boiling uncovered.

4 Pour the egg mixture all over the chicken. Cook gently, covered, for 4–5 minutes or until the eggs are set to your liking (I keep them quite soft). Sprinkle with the paprika and serve very hot.

Tagine of Chicken with Carrots

Tajen Djaj bel Khizü

The best carrots to use for this tagine are fresh garden ones with leafy tops. This dish is just as good served at room temperature. I often prepare it for summer picnics.
Serves 4–6

1 Put the chicken pieces in a large, deep sauté pan. Add the onion, garlic, parsley, spices, sea salt to taste, and ½ teaspoon pepper. Cover with water (about 3 cups) and pour in the olive oil. Bring to a boil over a medium-high heat, then cover and let boil for 30 minutes.

2 Add the carrots and most of the cilantro. Pour in the lemon juice. Reduce the heat to medium-low and cook, covered, for a further 15 minutes or until both chicken and carrots are done and the sauce has thickened. If you are using the olives, add them for the last 5 minutes of cooking.

3 Transfer the chicken pieces to a serving dish. Remove and discard the skin, if you like. If the sauce is too runny, increase the heat to high and boil uncovered until it becomes very concentrated. Scatter the carrots and olives around the chicken and pour the sauce all over. Garnish with the reserved cilantro and serve immediately.

1 free-range chicken (about 3¼ pounds) *cut into 8 pieces*

1 medium-sized onion *minced*

3 garlic cloves *minced*

1 bunch fresh flat-leaf parsley *most of bottom stems discarded, then minced (about ¾ cup)*

pinch of saffron filaments *crushed*

¾ teaspoon ground ginger

sea salt and finely ground black pepper

2 tablespoons extra virgin olive oil

1¾ pounds carrots *sliced into medium-thick rounds*

a few sprigs of cilantro *minced*

juice of ½ lemon, or to taste

⅔ cup black or purple olives (optional)

Tagine of Chicken with Olives and Preserved Lemon

Tajen Djaj Mchermel

This is one of the signature dishes of Morocco, and you are offered it everywhere—on the streets, in private homes, and in restaurants. It can be prepared using three of the four basic tagine sauces: mchermel, *as in the recipe below,* mqalli, *where the sauce is flavored with saffron, ginger, and pepper, or* mhammar, *where the only seasonings are cumin and paprika and the chicken is browned in the oven after it has stewed. The fourth sauce, which is not used in this tagine, is* kdra; *it is made with onion, pepper, and saffron.* **Serves 4–6**

1 garlic clove *minced*

½ teaspoon ground ginger

¼ teaspoon each ground cumin and paprika

pinch of saffron filaments *crushed*

sea salt and finely ground black pepper

1 free-range chicken (about 3¼ pounds)

2 medium-sized onions *thinly sliced*

1 bunch fresh flat-leaf parsley and cilantro *most of bottom stems discarded, then minced (about ¾ cup each)*

1 cinnamon stick

2 tablespoons extra virgin olive oil

2 tablespoons butter

juice of ½ lemon, or to taste

1 large preserved lemon, peel only *cut lengthwise into strips*

1 cup green and/or purple olives

1 Put the garlic, ginger, cumin, paprika, saffron, a little salt, and ¼ teaspoon pepper in a large Dutch oven. Mix together. Add the chicken and rub it well inside and out with the spice mixture.

2 Add the onions and herbs. Half cover with water (about 3½ cups) and drop in the cinnamon stick. Bring to a boil over medium-high heat, then add the oil and butter. Cover and let boil for 45 minutes or until the chicken is cooked.

3 Transfer the chicken to a plate and keep warm. Discard the cinnamon stick. Boil the broth uncovered for a further 10 minutes, stirring regularly, until concentrated. Add the lemon juice, preserved lemon peel, and olives and simmer for a few more minutes.

4 About 5 minutes before the sauce is ready, cut up the chicken neatly into 8 pieces (remove the skin if you like), then return to the pan, turning the pieces carefully in the sauce. Taste and adjust the seasoning if necessary. Transfer to a serving dish and serve very hot.

Couscous

Kseksü

Ideally, you should have a couscoussière *to steam couscous, although you can improvise with a normal steamer (if the holes are too big, line with a thin layer of muslin or cheesecloth). There is really no comparison between regular couscous and the pre-cooked, "instant" kind—regular couscous is much finer and has a slight crunch even when you reheat it—so always use regular couscous if you can.* **Serves 4–6**

3 cups very fine or fine couscous

sea salt

1 tablespoon extra virgin olive oil

2 tablespoons butter *melted*

1 Put the couscous in a shallow mixing bowl. Dissolve 1 teaspoon salt in ¼ cup water and sprinkle over the couscous. Stir with your fingers, rubbing to separate the grains and break up any lumps. When the couscous has soaked up all the water, stir in the oil.

2 Put the couscous in the top of the *couscoussière* and set over the bottom part (filled with boiling water or the broth to be served with the couscous; see recipes on pages 75–7). No steam should escape from the bottom pan, so, if necessary, wrap a strip of cloth around the edge of the pan before slotting in the steamer top. Steam the couscous, covered, for 20 minutes.

3 Tip the couscous into a bowl and sprinkle with a further ¼ cup water. Add the melted butter and stir well with a wooden spoon. Cover with a clean dish towel and leave for 15 minutes to fluff up.

4 Put the couscous back into the top part of the *couscoussière* and set over the pan of boiling liquid. Steam, uncovered, for a further 10–15 minutes (or the last 10–15 minutes of the cooking time of the broth). Tip the couscous into a large serving bowl. Taste and add more salt or butter if necessary, then arrange into a mound. Garnish according to the recipe you are using and serve.

Couscous with Monkfish

Kseksü bel Hüt

Monkfish has a firm, delicious flesh that is difficult to overcook, and it works very well in a couscous sauce. You can use other types of fish, such as conger eel or cod, but adjust the cooking time accordingly. If using pre-cooked couscous, prepare it according to the package directions, then steam it uncovered over the sauce in step 4. **Serves 4–6**

1 Pour 6 tablespoons of the oil into the bottom half of a *couscoussière* and place over medium-high heat. Dip the monkfish in flour and fry for 1 minute on each side to sear. Remove to a plate and set aside.

2 Sauté the onions and garlic in the same oil until lightly golden. Add the chopped tomatoes, the fish bone, thyme, parsley, cumin, paprika, and crushed chilies. Pour in 3½ cups water and add sea salt to taste. Bring to a boil, then add the butter and saffron.

3 Start preparing the couscous now, following the instructions in step 1 on page 74. Put the couscous into the top of the *couscoussière*, set it over the boiling broth, and steam, covered, for 20 minutes.

4 Tip the couscous into a bowl and add water and butter as instructed in step 3 on page 74; set aside. Carry on boiling the sauce, covered, for a further 15 minutes or until quite thick. Discard the fish bone, then reduce the heat to low and add the fish pieces. Place the couscous over the sauce and steam, uncovered, for 10–15 minutes or until both fish and couscous are done.

5 Meanwhile, mix the basil with the remaining oil and a little sea salt. Tip the couscous into a serving bowl and stir in the basil. Remove the fish from the tomato sauce and arrange over the couscous. Spoon a little sauce over the fish and serve immediately, with more sauce along side.

9 tablespoons extra virgin olive oil

1 monkfish tail (1¾ pounds) *boned (keep the bone) and cut into 6–8 pieces*

all-purpose flour *for coating*

3 medium-sized onions *thinly sliced*

3 garlic cloves *minced*

2 x 28-ounce cans Italian plum tomatoes *drained, seeded, and coarsely chopped*

1 tablespoon fresh thyme leaves

1 bunch fresh flat-leaf parsley *most of bottom stems discarded, then minced (about ¼ cup)*

1½ teaspoons ground cumin

1 teaspoon paprika

¼ teaspoon dried hot chili peppers crushed to a coarse powder, or to taste

sea salt

2 tablespoons butter

pinch of saffron filaments *crushed*

3 cups couscous

a handful of fresh basil leaves *minced*

Squabs Stuffed with Couscous

Hamam M'ammar bel Kseksü

In Morocco, pigeons, which can be quite tiny, are considered a delicacy. They are sold live in the markets, at rather high prices. This delicious couscous filling suits most small birds, both farmed and wild (if you cannot get squabs, the specially reared young pigeons, you can substitute poussins, although these tend to lack flavor). If you want to use pre-cooked couscous, prepare following the package directions; when the couscous has absorbed all the water, stir in 2 tablespoons melted butter and sea salt to taste. **Serves 4**

1 Prepare the couscous following the recipe on page 74, halving the amount of water, salt, and oil but not that of butter. Stop after step 3.

2 Put the cooled couscous in a mixing bowl. Add the almonds, raisins or dates, sugar, ginger, and ¼ teaspoon pepper and mix well together. Adjust the seasoning, and add more melted butter if the mixture seems dry. Fill the squabs with as much of the couscous mixture as they will take. Sew up the openings and place in a large Dutch oven.

3 Add the onion, saffron, *ras el hanout*, and a little sea salt and half cover with water (about 3½ cups). Bring to a boil over medium-high heat. Drop in the unsalted butter, then cover and leave to boil for 30 minutes. Reduce the heat to medium-low and carry on cooking, covered, for another 30 minutes or until the birds are tender and the sauce has thickened. Carefully turn the birds in the sauce regularly during cooking, and add a little water if the sauce is becoming too thick. If the sauce is too runny, raise the heat and boil uncovered until reduced.

4 About 10–15 minutes before the birds are ready, put the remaining couscous in the top half of a *coussoussière* or steamer, and steam, uncovered, over boiling water to finish. Transfer the squabs to a serving platter and spoon over the sauce. Serve hot, with the rest of the couscous.

1½ cups fine couscous

melted butter

¾ cup blanched almonds *coarsely chopped in a food processor*

1 heaping cup golden raisins or finely diced dates

1½ tablespoons confectioners' sugar

1 teaspoon ground ginger

sea salt and finely ground black pepper

4 squabs

1 medium-sized onion *thinly sliced*

pinch of saffron filaments *crushed*

1 teaspoon *ras el hanout*

4 tablespoons unsalted butter

Couscous with Seven Vegetables

Kseksü Bidawi

Most Moroccans prefer their couscous with lamb or chicken, but if they cannot afford meat they will make this vegetarian version. The choice of vegetables can be varied: pumpkin, artichoke hearts, peas, sweet potatoes, or whatever is in season can be substituted for any of those listed below. You can use pre-cooked couscous if you prefer, prepared according to the package directions. **Serves 4–6**

¼ cup dried chick peas
soaked overnight with ½ teaspoon baking soda added to the water

pinch of saffron filaments *crushed*

2 medium-sized onions *quartered*

3 medium-sized ripe tomatoes
peeled and coarsely chopped

sea salt and finely ground black pepper

3 tablespoons extra virgin olive oil

6 tablespoons unsalted butter

3 cups couscous

heart of ½ small head cabbage
cut in 4 lengthwise and cored

5 ounces each carrots and zucchini *halved lengthwise, cored, and cut into 2-inch pieces*

5 ounces turnips *quartered*

5 ounces shelled fava beans, fresh or frozen

a few sprigs each of fresh flat-leaf parsley and cilantro *minced*

⅓ cup golden raisins

¼ teaspoon dried hot chili peppers crushed to a coarse powder (optional)

1 Drain the chick peas, rinse them well, and put into the bottom part of a *couscoussière* or steamer. Add the saffron, onions, tomatoes, 6¼ cups water, and 2 teaspoons pepper. Bring to a boil, then add the olive oil and 4 tablespoons of the butter. Cover and leave to boil for 30 minutes. Meanwhile, start preparing the couscous, following the instructions on page 74, and set on top of the boiling vegetables for the first steaming.

2 Add the cabbage to the stew in the *couscoussière* or steamer and cook, covered, for a further 15 minutes.

3 Add the rest of the vegetables, together with the herbs, raisins, and salt to taste. Put the prepared couscous into the top of the *couscoussière*, set it over the boiling broth, and steam, uncovered, for 10–15 minutes or until the vegetables are ready.

4 Transfer the couscous to a serving dish and stir in the remaining butter. Taste the broth and adjust the seasoning, if necessary. Arrange the vegetables on top of the couscous and sprinkle with some of the broth. Pour the rest of the broth into a separate bowl and stir in the crushed chilies, if using. Serve immediately. In Morocco, where everybody eats straight from the serving dish, people pour enough broth over the couscous nearest to them to moisten it to taste.

Calf's Foot with Chick Peas and Wheat

Hergma

For Moroccans, this is classic street breakfast fare, and huge enamelware dishes filled with this rich mixture of chick peas and calf's foot are a common early-morning sight. Though I love calf's foot, I couldn't find this dish appetizing on the streets. Luckily a friend agreed to make it for me, for lunch, and it was perfectly exquisite. You can replace the calf's foot with sheep's feet, in which case allow at least one per person. **Serves 4–6**

1 If the wheat berries are not husked, soak overnight in water.

2 Put the cleaned pieces of calf's foot in a large Dutch oven and pour in 3 quarts water. Bring to a boil over medium-high heat, then skim, cover, and leave to boil for 45 minutes.

3 Add the rinsed and drained chick peas and wheat berries, the oil, peeled garlic cloves, cumin, and crushed chilies. Boil, covered, for 1½ hours, stirring occasionally, until the meat is tender and the broth has reduced to an unctuous sauce.

4 Add sea salt to taste. If the sauce is still runny, increase the heat to high and boil, uncovered, until reduced. Stir in the paprika. Taste and adjust the seasoning if necessary, then serve very hot with good bread and a selection of refreshing salads.

¾ cup husked wheat berries

2 calf's feet *singed, thoroughly washed and cut across in half (ask your butcher to do this for you)*

1¼ cups dried chick peas *soaked overnight with 1 teaspoon baking soda added to the water*

6 tablespoons extra virgin olive oil

4 garlic cloves

2 tablespoons ground cumin

¼ teaspoon dried hot chili peppers crushed to a coarse powder, or to taste

sea salt

2 tablespoons paprika

SIDE
DISHES

New Potatoes with Parsley and Garlic

Btata Mqalliyya

Here is a simple way of giving plain boiled potatoes a lift. The saffron gives the skins a pale yellow tinge and, together with the parsley and garlic, enhances their flavor. You can prepare Jerusalem artichokes the same way. If they are small, halve the amount of water and cook for 10 minutes only. **Serves 4**

2 tablespoons extra virgin olive oil

2 garlic cloves *minced*

1 pound new potatoes

a few sprigs of fresh flat-leaf parsley *minced*

pinch of saffron filaments *crushed*

sea salt and finely ground black pepper

1 Put all the ingredients in a medium-sized saucepan, seasoning with a little salt and ¼ teaspoon pepper, and add ¾ cup water.

2 Bring to a boil over medium-high heat, then cover and leave to boil for 15–20 minutes, stirring the potatoes halfway through, or until the potatoes are tender and the sauce has reduced. If necessary, increase the heat to high and boil uncovered until reduced. Serve hot, warm, or at room temperature.

Braised Turnips with Raisins
Mahfür bel Zbib

This preparation also works well with sweet potatoes, although the combination of flavors and textures is a little less delicate. If you use sweet potatoes, reduce the cooking time to 10–15 minutes and use only 1 cup water. **Serves 4**

8 small turnips (about 1½ pounds) *peeled and quartered*

1 cup golden raisins

1 medium-sized onion *thinly sliced*

scant ¼ teaspoon dried hot chili peppers crushed to a coarse powder, or to taste

1 teaspoon paprika

sea salt to taste

3 tablespoons extra virgin olive oil

1 Put all the ingredients in a saucepan and add 1½ cups water. Bring to a boil over medium-high heat, then cover and leave to boil for 10 minutes.

2 Reduce the heat to medium-low and cook for a further 5–10 minutes or until the turnips are done to your liking and the water has evaporated. If necessary, increase the heat to high and boil uncovered until reduced. Taste and adjust the seasoning. Serve hot.

Spiced Onions with Honey

Besla M'assala

This surprising dish does not have a very appealing color—the spice mixture turns the onions dark brown—but don't be put off, because it is quite luscious. Traditionally it is served with plain fried fish, but it is particularly good with Squabs Stuffed with Couscous (page 77). **Serves 4**

1 Put the oil and onions in a large sauté pan, add 1½ cups water and place over medium-high heat. Stir in the *ras el hanout* and a little sea salt. Bring to a boil, then cover and leave to boil for 15 minutes. Reduce the heat to medium-low and simmer, stirring regularly, until the onions become quite mushy. This will take 20–30 minutes.

2 Uncover the pan, increase the heat a little, and cook, stirring continuously, for about 5 minutes to reduce the sauce further, if needed. Add the honey and leave to bubble for a few more minutes. Taste and adjust the seasoning if necessary. Serve very hot.

¼ cup extra virgin olive oil

6 medium-sized onions (2 pounds) *thinly sliced*

1½ teaspoons *ras el hanout*

sea salt

2 tablespoons good honey

Tomatoes Stuffed with Grated Vegetables

Matecha M'ammara

An unusually plain dish, here the only spice used is chili, instead of the more usual mix of cumin and paprika. You can omit the chili, or reduce the amount, if you don't like hot tastes. The vegetables will still be delicious. **Serves 4–6**

1 Use 1 tablespoon olive oil to grease a baking dish large enough to hold all the tomato halves. Arrange the tomato halves in the dish, cut side up. Sprinkle with a little salt.

2 Put the zucchini, onion, and garlic in a mixing bowl. Add the herbs, chilies, and salt to taste and mix well together. Taste and adjust the seasoning if necessary. Cover each tomato half with 3 tablespoons of the vegetable mixture. If there is any filling left over, divide it equally among the tomatoes.

3 Drizzle about ½ tablespoon olive oil over each tomato half. Bake in a preheated oven at 300°F for 1½–2 hours or until the vegetables have cooked to the degree you prefer (after 1½ hours they will still have a slight crunch). Spoon the cooking juices over the filling and leave to cool before transferring the tomatoes to a serving platter. Serve warm or at room temperature, with more olive oil and crushed chilies for those who want them.

5 tablespoons extra virgin olive oil

4 large, firm, vine-ripened tomatoes *cut in half horizontally*

sea salt

1 pound zucchini *grated (about 4 cups)*

1 medium-sized onion *very thinly sliced*

1 garlic clove *minced*

1 bunch each fresh flat-leaf parsley and cilantro *most of bottom stems discarded, then minced (about ¾ cup each)*

scant ½ teaspoon dried hot chili peppers crushed to a coarse powder, or to taste

Lentils with Swiss Chard

'Adess bil Silq

I had the best version of this dish in a narrow den in the medina *of Tetouan, where the cooking range consisted of six charcoal-fire burners. Cooking over charcoal fires is still very common in Morocco, but I had not seen such a well-organized range anywhere else in the country. It was manned by a rather handsome, gaunt man who looked more like an artist than a cook. His food was particularly refined, and this is his recipe. If you can't find Swiss chard, use young leaf spinach instead, which you should leave whole. The taste will not be as distinctive, but it will still be good.* **Serves 4–6**

1½ cups large green lentils

1 pound Swiss chard, leaves only *shredded into thin strips*

2 bunches cilantro *most of bottom stems discarded, then minced (about 1½ cups)*

1 medium-sized onion *thinly sliced*

¼ cup olive oil

1½ teaspoons ground cumin

1 teaspoon paprika

sea salt and finely ground black pepper

juice of 1 lemon, or to taste

1 Put the lentils in a large saucepan and cover with water (about 5 cups). Bring to a boil over medium-high heat. Cover the pan and boil for 15 minutes.

2 Stir in the Swiss chard, cilantro, and onion. Cover and cook for 5 minutes or until the chard has wilted. Stir in the olive oil, cumin, paprika, and ½ teaspoon pepper. Boil, covered, for a further 10 minutes or until the lentils are tender and the sauce is reduced. Stir from time to time to make sure the lentils are not sticking and to blend the leaves in evenly. If the mixture becomes too dry, add a little water. If it is too runny, increase the heat to high and boil uncovered until reduced.

3 Add the lemon juice and salt to taste and cook for another minute or two. Taste and adjust the seasoning if necessary, then serve hot, warm, or at room temperature.

Artichoke Hearts and Rice

Qoq bel Rozz

Artichokes are a very popular vegetable in Morocco, particularly a wild variety, which has striking spiky leaves. Both the stalks and flower head of this wild artichoke are eaten, and the choke is dried and added in small quantities to milk to produce a curdled drink.
Serves 4

1 If using fresh artichokes, first prepare each heart by removing most of the stem and cutting off the tops of the leaves. Pull off all the leaves, and peel the sides until you get to the heart, then use a teaspoon to scoop out the hairy choke. Trim the dark green parts from the base, and cut the hearts into quarters (if they are large, cut them into 6 wedges). Keep the pieces in water with a little lemon juice added to prevent them from turning brown. If using frozen artichoke hearts, thaw by plunging them in boiling water, then cut them into pieces and keep in acidulated water as for fresh ones.

2 Put the artichoke hearts in a saucepan, add the rest of the ingredients, seasoning with a little salt and ¼ teaspoon pepper, and cover with water (about 1¼ cups). Bring to a boil, then cover and reduce the heat to low. Simmer for 15–20 minutes or until the rice has absorbed the liquid.

3 Wrap the lid with a clean dish towel, replace it on the pan, and leave to sit for 5 minutes before serving.

4 large or 8 small artichokes, or use 14 ounces frozen artichoke hearts

juice of 1 lemon

¾ cup white short-grain rice

3 garlic cloves *minced*

2 tablespoons fresh thyme leaves

pinch of saffron filaments *crushed*

3 tablespoons extra virgin olive oil

sea salt and finely ground black pepper

Okra in Tomato Sauce

Maraq bel-Melükhiyya

If you are using fresh okra, choose them quite small and unblemished—larger ones are normally rather stringy and not as tasty. Frozen okra are always small, but they do not have as fine a taste or texture as fresh okra. **Serves 4**

1 pound okra (fresh or frozen)

3 tablespoons extra virgin olive oil

1 garlic clove *minced*

1 x 16-ounce can Italian plum tomatoes *coarsely chopped with their juice*

½ bunch each fresh flat-leaf parsley and cilantro *most of bottom stems discarded, then minced (about ⅓ cup each)*

½ teaspoon ground cumin

1 teaspoon paprika

¼ teaspoon dried hot chili peppers crushed to a coarse powder, or to taste

sea salt

1 If you are using fresh okra, shave the stems off, following the slant; make sure you don't break into the seed part of the vegetable, which is where the dreaded mucilagenous substance lurks. Wash and dry well. If you are using frozen okra, thaw them by plunging in boiling water, then drain and pat dry.

2 Heat the oil in a Dutch oven over medium-high heat and fry the minced garlic until golden. Add the okra and sauté for 2–3 minutes. This should seal them and make them less gooey.

3 Add the chopped tomatoes with their juice, the herbs, spices, and salt to taste and bring to a boil. Cover and leave to boil for 10 minutes.

4 Reduce the heat to medium-low and simmer for a further 5 minutes or until the okra is tender and the sauce has thickened. Serve hot, warm, or at room temperature.

Fennel Purée

Besbass Methün

This purée is usually prepared with the yellow buds and stalks of wild fennel when it is in bloom in early spring. The fennel is picked in abandoned fields, bunched up, and sold in town or village markets. The preparation of the buds and stalks is quite time-consuming: both have to be peeled and then cooked for rather a long time before being mashed up and sautéed. But the dish can also be made with ordinary bulb fennel. Be sure to cook the fennel until it is really soft. **Serves 4**

5 fennel bulbs (3 pounds)

3 garlic cloves

juice of 1 lemon

3 tablespoons extra virgin olive oil

1 teaspoon paprika

⅛ teaspoon dried hot chili peppers crushed to a coarse powder, or to taste

½ teaspoon ground cumin

sea salt

To serve:

½ preserved lemon, peel only
cut lengthwise into strips

1 Trim the fennel bulbs, removing any hard outer leaves, and cut into quarters lengthwise. Put into the top half of a steamer with the peeled garlic cloves. Pour the lemon juice all over the fennel, so that it does not discolor, then cover and steam for 40 minutes or until very tender.

2 Process the cooked fennel and garlic through the coarse grater of a food processor or mash with a potato masher. Leave for 5 minutes, then drain off the liquid that has seeped out.

3 Heat the oil in a frying pan. Add the mashed fennel, spices, and sea salt to taste and simmer over low heat, stirring regularly, until the purée has thickened. This should take 10–15 minutes. Taste and adjust the seasoning if necessary. Garnish with the preserved lemon strips and serve hot, warm, or at room temperature.

Pumpkin Purée

Gar'a Hamra

Pumpkins are an important part of the winter diet of the Berbers in the High Atlas mountains, and this sweet-spicy purée is often served with a chicken tagine (tajen m'derbel) on the first day after the end of Ramadan. For a plain salty version, you can omit the cinnamon and honey, and use argan oil instead of olive oil to give the purée a nutty taste. **Serves 4**

1 Fill a saucepan with water, place over high heat, and bring to a boil. Drop in the pumpkin pieces and cook for 5 minutes, or until they are soft. Drain the pumpkin in a colander.

2 Pour the oil into the pan and place over low heat. When the oil is hot, return the pumpkin pieces to the pan and stir and mash them until you have a smooth, slightly darker purée.

3 Season with the cinnamon, a little sea salt, and a pinch of pepper, and stir in the honey. Simmer for a few more minutes, still stirring. Taste and adjust the seasoning if necessary. Serve hot, warm, or at room temperature.

1 small pumpkin (about 3 pounds) *peeled, seeded, and cut into medium-sized chunks*

5 tablespoons extra virgin olive oil

¼ teaspoon ground cinnamon

sea salt and finely ground black pepper

2 tablespoons good honey

Sautéed Purée of Herbs

Baqüla

I was lucky to spot this dish before the stall-holder had finished covering it with olives. It is the summer version of baqüla, *which is traditionally made with mallow, a winter herb. This one is prepared with purslane or spinach, with various other herbs, and I was keen to taste it so I could make it at home where mallow is unobtainable. You will need an enormous quantity of herbs for this recipe, but it is well worth the trouble. The best places to buy herbs in such quantities are Middle Eastern or Indian markets.* **Serves 4**

2¾ pounds purslane, leaves only or 1¼ pounds spinach *shredded into strips*

14 ounces each fresh flat-leaf parsley and cilantro (about 7 bunches each) *most of bottom stems discarded, then coarsely chopped (about 5 cups each)*

1 cup coarsely chopped fresh mint leaves

3 garlic cloves *minced*

5 tablespoons extra virgin olive oil

scant ½ teaspoon dried hot chili peppers crushed to a coarse powder

juice of 3 lemons, or to taste

sea salt

1½ teaspoons each ground cumin and paprika

To serve:

½ preserved lemon, peel only *cut lengthwise into strips*

⅓ cup black or purple olives

1 Put the purslane or shredded spinach, parsley, cilantro, mint, and garlic in the top part of a steamer. Steam for 5–7 minutes or until wilted.

2 Heat the olive oil in a large frying pan over high heat. Add the steamed herbs and garlic, the chilies, lemon juice, and salt to taste. Sauté for 10–15 minutes or until the cooking juices have evaporated, stirring regularly. Stir in the cumin and paprika, and leave to cool.

3 Transfer the cooked herbs to a shallow serving bowl. Garnish with the strips of preserved lemon and olives, forming alternate lines. Serve at room temperature.

Fried Eggplants

Boudenjal Maqli

Fried vegetables are an essential part of street food. In most stalls you will find trays of fried eggplant slices and whole green sweet peppers (the long, thin variety) alongside the salads. You can have fried eggplants on their own with bread, or, more usually, as an accompaniment to grilled meat or fried fish. Sometimes they are used as a garnish to plain meat tagines. The addition of a lemon, parsley, and garlic sauce gives the eggplants a particularly delectable and almost refreshing taste. **Serves 4**

1 Peel the eggplants lengthwise, leaving thin strips of skin, then cut across into rounds about ½ inch thick. Sprinkle with salt and leave to sweat for 15–30 minutes. Rinse under cold water and pat dry with paper towels.

2 Mix the lemon juice with the garlic, chopped parsley, ¼ teaspoon pepper, and a little sea salt.

3 Heat enough vegetable oil to deep-fry the eggplants in a large frying pan. When the oil is very hot (when you dip in an eggplant slice, the oil should bubble around it), fry the eggplants for 1–2 minutes on each side or until soft and golden all over. Remove with a slotted spoon to several layers of paper towel to drain. (Press 1 or 2 layers of paper towel on top to extract the maximum oil.)

4 Transfer the fried eggplants to a serving platter and pour the lemon sauce all over. Serve warm or at room temperature.

2 eggplants (about 10 ounces each)

sea salt and finely ground black pepper

juice of 1 lemon, or to taste

1 garlic clove *minced*

3–4 sprigs of fresh flat-leaf parsley *minced*

vegetable oil for deep-frying

97

Potato Cakes with Cilantro

Ma'qüda

Here are potato cakes with a difference. They have a strong taste of cumin, paprika, and herbs, and a delicately crisp skin because of the egg coating. If you think the mash sounds too spicy, reduce the seasonings to your taste. The potato cakes are perfect for picnics.

Makes about 12 cakes

1 **pound potatoes**

2 unpeeled garlic cloves

a few sprigs each of fresh flat-leaf parsley and cilantro *minced*

1½ teaspoons each ground cumin and paprika

¼ teaspoon dried hot chili peppers crushed to a coarse powder, or to taste

sea salt

3 medium free-range eggs

vegetable oil for frying

1 Put the unpeeled potatoes and garlic in a pan, cover with water, and bring to a boil. Cook for 20 minutes or until they are tender. Drain and cool slightly.

2 Peel the potatoes, and slip the garlic out of their skins. Mash together. Add the herbs, spices, and a little salt, then taste and adjust the seasoning if necessary. Mix in 2 of the eggs until well blended. Shape into small round cakes about ⅝ inch thick and 3 inches in diameter.

3 Beat the remaining egg in a shallow dish.

4 Pour enough vegetable oil to shallow-fry the potato cakes into a large frying pan and place over medium-high heat. When the oil is hot, dip the potato cakes in the egg to coat both sides, then slip into the oil. Fry for about 1–2 minutes on each side or until lightly golden. Remove to several layers of paper towel to drain. Serve hot, warm, or at room temperature.

Spicy Cilantro Fritters

Chermüla Beignets

It is said that fritters are of Saracen origin and that they were brought to the West by the Crusaders. These crispy fritters are usually made with the leftover chermüla *marinade for fried fish. They are so tasty, though, that they are worth making on their own to serve with cocktails or as an appetizer. If you are going to serve them before dinner, drop the batter into the hot oil by the teaspoonful to make small* bouchées. **Makes 20–25 fritters**

chermüla **(see Fried Fish with Spicy Cilantro Sauce, page 46)**

1 free-range egg

1 cup all-purpose flour

½ teaspoon rapid-rise dry yeast

vegetable oil for deep-frying

1 Combine the *chermüla* with the egg, whisking well to mix. Add the flour and yeast. Stir in ½ cup tepid water to make a batter, then leave in a warm place for 45 minutes to become bubbly.

2 Heat enough vegetable oil in a large frying pan to deep-fry the fritters. When the oil is very hot (it is hot enough when the oil forms bubbles around a tiny bit of batter), drop in the batter by the tablespoonful. Leave a little space between each fritter so that they don't stick to each other, and fry just a few at a time. Fry for 1–2 minutes on each side or until golden brown all over. Remove to several layers of paper towel to drain. Serve hot, on their own or with fried fish.

The Chicken That Flew

Djaja Tarat

The amusing name of this vegetarian dish suggests that the chicken decided to fly out of the pot rather than be cooked with the vegetables. I am not sure why this recipe has such an evocative title, but I love the sound of it as well as its unexpected combination of flavors.
Serves 4

1 Drain and rinse the chick peas well, then put in a saucepan. Add the crushed saffron and 1 quart water. Bring to a boil over medium-high heat, then cover and leave to boil for 35 minutes or until the chick peas are quite tender.

2 Add the sweet potato, onion, cilantro, oil, salt to taste, and scant ½ teaspoon pepper. Cook, covered, for a further 10 minutes or until the sweet potatoes are tender and the water has evaporated. If the sauce is still runny, increase the heat to high and boil uncovered until reduced. Serve hot, warm, or at room temperature.

¾ cup dried chick peas *soaked overnight with ½ teaspoon baking soda added to the water*

pinch of saffron filaments *crushed*

1 large orange-fleshed sweet potato (14 ounces) *peeled and cut into small chunks*

1 medium-sized onion *thinly sliced*

1 bunch cilantro *most of bottom stems discarded, then minced (about ¾ cup)*

2 tablespoons extra virgin olive oil

sea salt and finely ground black pepper

Cannellini Beans with Saffron

Fassülya Kdra

This is one of the most popular of Moroccan street-food dishes—you find it everywhere, from north to south, and even in the desert. The beans are often ladled on top of a plain meat or variety-meat stew. I suspect that the street vendors often economize and use turmeric instead of saffron to give the dish its typical pale yellow color, but I prefer saffron, which also adds a subtle and unusual flavor. **Serves 4–6**

1 Drain the beans, rinse well, and put into a large saucepan. Add the crushed saffron. Cover with water (about 1½ quarts) and bring to a boil. Add the butter, then cover and leave to boil over medium-high heat for 30 minutes.

2 Add the onions, parsley, and 1 teaspoon pepper and stir to mix. Reduce the heat to medium-low and leave to bubble, covered, for another 30 minutes or until the beans are tender. Stir from time to time to make sure the beans are not sticking.

3 Just before the beans are ready, add salt to taste. If the sauce is too thick, add a little water. Taste and adjust the seasoning if necessary. Serve hot, warm, or at room temperature.

3 cups dried cannellini beans *soaked overnight with ½ teaspoon baking soda added to the water*

2 good pinches of saffron filaments *crushed*

7 tablespoons unsalted butter

3 medium-sized onions *thinly sliced*

½ bunch fresh flat-leaf parsley *most of bottom stems discarded, then minced (about ⅓ cup)*

sea salt and finely ground white pepper

Sweet Grated Carrot Salad
Khizü Mehqüq

Khizü Mehqüq *is generally eaten after the main course and before the dessert, to refresh the palate. Adding sugar to salads is a specialty of Casablanca, and carrots—like beets or cucumber—lend themselves particularly well to sweet seasonings.* **Serves 4–6**

4–6 sprigs of fresh flat-leaf parsley *most of bottom stems discarded, then minced*

¼ teaspoon ground cinnamon

1½ tablespoons confectioners' sugar

juice of 2 oranges

1¾ pounds carrots *grated*

1 Mix the chopped parsley with the cinnamon, sugar, and orange juice in a salad bowl.

2 Add the grated carrots and mix well together. Taste and adjust the seasoning if necesssary. Serve slightly chilled.

Grated Cucumber Salad

Khiyar Mehqüq

This refreshing sour-sweet salad is particularly fine when prepared with feggüs, *a ridged, native cucumber that is less watery and more crunchy than regular cucumber. In the summer you can find this kind of cucumber in Lebanese and other Middle Eastern markets (the Lebanese / Syrian variety is smaller than the Moroccan, and is called* meqteh).

Serves 4

1 Put the grated cucumber in a colander, stir in the salt, and leave for at least half an hour to drain off the excess liquid.

2 Transfer the grated cucumber to a salad bowl. Add the remaining ingredients and mix well together. Taste and adjust the seasoning if necessary. Leave the salad to stand for about 15 minutes to allow the cucumber to absorb the seasoning before serving slightly chilled.

2¼ pounds small cucumbers
peeled, seeded, and grated

¼ teaspoon sea salt

1 tablespoon fresh thyme leaves

1½ tablespoons confectioners' sugar

1½ tablespoons white wine vinegar

½ teaspoon caraway seeds

Beets Salad

Shlada del Barba bel Ma Zhar

This salad has a sweetish, fragrant taste, unusual in a vegetable mixture, but it is excellent. The beets are traditionally grated when mixed with the sweet dressing, but I find that grating cooked beets is too messy, so I prefer to dice them. **Serves 4–6**

1¾ pounds raw beets

2 tablespoons orange flower water

juice of ½ lemon, or to taste

¾ teaspoon paprika

scant ¼ teaspoon each ground cumin and cinnamon

1½ tablespoons confectioners' sugar

sea salt

1 Put the beets to boil for 1 hour or until they are tender. Or, if you prefer, you can bake them, in which case wrap them individually in aluminum foil and bake in a preheated oven at 350°F for 1 hour or until tender.

2 When the beets are cool enough to handle, peel and dice into small cubes (or grate, if you prefer).

3 Mix together the rest of the ingredients in a salad bowl. Add the beets and toss together. Taste and adjust the seasoning if necessary. Serve slightly chilled.

From left to right *Grated Cucumber Salad (page 105), Beets Salad, Sweet Grated Carrot Salad (page 104).*

DESSERTS

AND DRINKS

Moroccan Rice Pudding

Rozz bel hleeb

You will find rice pudding throughout the Middle East and North Africa, but the Moroccan version is a lot more runny than others. Many westerners find it hard to get used to fragrant flavorings, but the orange flower water imparts a delicate and sensuous taste to an otherwise plain pudding. **Serves 4**

¾ **cup white short-grain rice**

scant ¼ teaspoon sea salt

2 tablespoons unsalted butter

2½ cups milk

⅔ **cup confectioners' sugar**

2 tablespoons orange flower water

⅓ **cup blanched almonds** *sautéed in a little butter until golden*

1 Rinse the rice under cold water, then put it in a saucepan. Add 1½ cups water and the salt. Bring to a boil, then add the butter. Reduce the heat to low, cover, and simmer, stirring regularly, for 15 minutes or until the water is almost completely absorbed.

2 Add the milk and sugar and increase the heat to high. Bring back to a boil, then reduce the heat to medium and boil, uncovered, for 5 minutes or until the mixture has the consistency of runny oatmeal or porridge. Stir the rice regularly so that it does not stick. If you prefer a thicker texture, boil for a few minutes longer, but remember that the pudding will continue to thicken as it cools.

3 Add the orange flower water and let the mixture bubble for a few more minutes. Pour into a shallow serving bowl, cover with a clean cloth, and leave to cool. Just before serving, scatter the sautéed almonds all over the rice. Serve at room temperature or slightly chilled.

Moroccan Pancakes

Beghrir

These semolina pancakes are usually served for breakfast. They reheat very well in a low oven, so you can make them the night before and keep them covered until the next morning. You can also freeze them. If you prefer smaller pancakes, drop the batter into the pan by tablespoons. **Makes about 6 pancakes**

1 cup + 2 tablespoons fine semolina flour

⅓ cup all-purpose flour

1 teaspoon rapid-rise dry yeast

½ teaspoon sea salt

1 medium free-range egg

1¾ cups milk

To serve:

unsalted butter

good honey

1 Put the semolina, flour, yeast, and salt in a mixing bowl.

2 Beat the egg and incorporate it into the milk. Gradually stir the milk into the dry ingredients, then whisk for about 10 minutes or until you have a creamy batter. Cover with a clean cloth and leave in a warm place for 2 hours or until the batter is bubbly.

3 Grease a non-stick frying pan with a little vegetable oil and place over medium heat. When the pan is hot, pour in a ladleful of batter, and tip and rotate the pan to make a pancake 7–8 inches in diameter. Cook for 2 minutes, without turning, until the top has become dry and full of holes. The pancake will be smooth and golden on the cooked side. Remove to a cloth.

4 Continue making pancakes, oiling the pan again after the second and again after the fourth. Don't pile the pancakes on top of each other until they have completely cooled, to prevent them from sticking together. Serve hot with butter and honey.

Sweet Couscous

Seffa

This type of nearly sweet dish is described by Moroccans as avant les desserts *(before the desserts). Sweet couscous is served at the end of a meal, not so much as a dessert, but more as a semi-sweet finish before the fruits and tea are brought in. This couscous is also delicious for breakfast, although I doubt whether my Moroccan friends would approve.*

Serves 4–6

1 Prepare the couscous following the recipe instructions on page 74, using the oil and melted butter. When the couscous is done, leave it in the top part of the *couscoussière* or steamer.

2 Meanwhile, melt half the softened butter in a frying pan over medium-high heat. When the butter is hot, sauté the almonds until they are golden brown all over. Transfer to a plate and leave to cool. Coarsely grind two-thirds of the almonds in a blender. The remaining whole almonds will be used for the garnish.

3 Add the rest of the softened butter and the sugar to the hot couscous and mix well. Tip half of the couscous into a medium-sized shallow serving bowl and spread the ground almonds evenly on top. Sprinkle with a little extra confectioners' sugar, then cover with the remaining couscous.

4 Arrange the couscous into a mound with a pointed top. Sprinkle a little ground cinnamon into 4 thin lines that fan out from the top all the way down to the bottom. Line up the whole almonds in between the cinnamon trails. Serve while still hot, with extra confectioners' sugar and cinnamon for those who like it.

3 cups very fine or fine couscous

sea salt

1 tablespoon extra virgin olive oil

2 tablespoons unsalted butter
melted

4 tablespoons unsalted butter
softened

1 cup blanched almonds

3 tablespoons confectioners' sugar, plus extra for dusting

ground cinnamon

Orange and Cinnamon Salad

Laymün bel-Qerfa

In this simple salad, fragrant orange flower water adds a wonderfully exotic flavor. Sprinkle the cinnamon to taste—I prefer just a light dusting. **Serves 4–6**

1 Peel the oranges to expose the flesh, and cut them into medium-thin slices. Remove any pith. Arrange the slices on a serving platter, overlapping them slightly.

2 Stir the orange flower water into the orange juice and pour evenly over the orange slices. Sprinkle ground cinnamon lightly and evenly over the oranges just before serving.

2¼ pounds good oranges
slightly chilled

1 teaspoon orange flower water

juice of 1 orange

ground cinnamon

Tressed Pastries

Chbakiyya

These pastries are a staple throughout the month of Ramadan, and are most often served with the savory soup, Harira (page 16). Two people are normally involved in preparing chbakiyyas—one continuously kneads the dough while the other shapes, then fries the pastries. **Makes about 30 pastries**

1⅔ cups all-purpose plain flour

¾ cup sesame seeds *toasted, then half of the seeds finely ground*

pinch of sea salt

⅛ teaspoon ground cinnamon

1 teaspoon rapid-rise dry yeast

pinch of saffron filaments *crushed and infused in* **2 tablespoons orange flower water**

½ free-range egg *beaten*

1 tablespoon vinegar

3 tablespoons unsalted butter *melted* **plus extra for greasing**

vegetable oil for deep-frying

For the syrup:

2¼ pounds (about 3 cups) honey

4 small grains mastic (optional)

2 tablespoons orange flower water

1 Put the flour into a bowl and add the ground sesame seeds, salt, cinnamon, and yeast. Pour in the saffron water, egg, vinegar, and melted butter and work into the dry ingredients with your fingers. Gradually add about ¼–½ cup tepid water. Knead well for about 15 minutes.

2 Butter your working surface and rolling pin. Pinch off a piece of dough the size of a small orange and roll it out thinly (about ¹⁄₁₆ inch). Cut into strips about 4 inches long and ¾ inch wide. Lift 3 strips and press the top ends together. Braid the strips loosely and press the bottom ends together. Shape loosely into a round and press the ends well together. Continue shaping the pastries until you finish half the dough.

3 Pour enough vegetable oil to deep-fry the pastries into a large frying pan and place over high heat. Put the honey, mastic grains, and orange flower water in a deep saucepan and set over medium heat. When the honey starts bubbling, turn the heat down to low.

4 When the oil reaches 320°F, fry the pastries for 2 minutes on each side or until browned all over. Remove with a slotted spoon and drop into the hot honey syrup. Leave for a few minutes, then remove with a slotted spoon to a platter. Sprinkle on both sides with toasted sesame seeds and leave to cool. While you are frying the first batch of pastries, your "sous-chef" should be shaping the rest of the dough into pastries.

Moroccan Shortbread

Ghreyba

Some of the best ghreyba *I have ever eaten were made by a Berber woman in the* medina *in Essaouira. She squatted by a kaftan shop, selling her homemade* ghreybas *off a battered metal tray. I bought one and walked on. As I ate it I realized that it was totally scrumptious. I walked back. She was still sitting there, immutable. I bought another cookie. In the next 15 minutes I went back and forth several times, each time thinking it would be the last, but not able to resist her wonderful* ghreybas. *This is the recipe she gave me.*

Makes 30–35 biscuits

1 Put the sugar and powdered mastic in a mixing bowl and make a well in the center. Add the egg yolks and incorporate them into the sugar with the tips of your fingers.

2 Add the butter and blend it in well, then gradually add the flour. Knead the dough until it is smooth and firm. This will take about 5 minutes. Add a little more flour (up to ⅓ cup) if you think the dough is too soft.

3 Pinch off a piece of dough and roll it into a ball the size of a walnut. Flatten it on your palm, leaving the top quite rounded, to make a cookie measuring about 2 inches in diameter. If you like, press an almond in the middle, then place the cookie on a buttered baking sheet. Continue shaping the cookies until the dough is used up.

4 Bake in a preheated oven at 350°F for 15–20 minutes or until barely colored. Leave to cool briefly on the baking sheet before transferring the cookies to a wire rack. Stored in an airtight container, the cookies will keep for up to 2 weeks.

1¼ cups sugar

½ teaspoon mastic *crushed to a powder*

2 medium free-range egg yolks

1 cup + 2 tablespoons (2½ sticks) unsalted butter *softened*

3 cups all-purpose flour

⅓ cup blanched almonds (optional)

117

Pastry Crescents filled with Almond Paste

Qa'b el-Ghzal

Sometimes known as cornes de gazelles, *these are normally served in the afternoon with mint tea or offered at the end of fancy dinners.* **Makes about 40 pastries**

For the filling:

3½ cups blanched almonds *soaked in boiling water for 15–20 minutes, then drained and dried*

1¼ cups confectioners' sugar, plus extra for dusting

¼ cup orange flower water

2 tablespoons unsalted butter *softened* **plus extra for greasing**

½ teaspoon mastic *crushed to a powder* **(optional)**

For the pastry:

1⅔ cups all-purpose flour

2 tablespoons unsalted butter *melted*

1 Put the almonds and sugar in a food processor and process to a very fine paste. Transfer to a bowl. Add the orange flower water, butter, and mastic, if using, and mix with your hands to a paste. Cover and set aside.

2 Put the flour in a shallow mixing bowl and make a well in the middle. Pour in the melted butter and gradually add ½–¾ cup water, working it in with your fingers. Knead for 15 minutes, until the dough is smooth with a slightly looser consistency than that of bread dough.

3 Divide the almond paste into 40 pieces. Roll each into a ball and then into a small sausage about 4 inches long with tapering ends.

4 Smear your pastry board, rolling pin, and hands with butter. Take about half of the dough at a time and roll it out, turning it over once or twice, into a very thin strip about 5 inches wide. Carefully stretch the dough with your hands to widen and thin it a little more, then place an almond paste sausage at one end, about ¾ inch from the edge. Fold the dough tightly over the almond paste and pinch the filling upward and sideways, bending it at the same time, to form a crescent. Press the edges together and cut, following the shape of the crescent, using a fluted pastry wheel. The crescent should measure about 4 inches long and 1 inch high. Prick with a needle on both sides and place on a buttered baking sheet. Repeat the process, using the rest of the dough to make 20 crescents.

5 Bake in a preheated oven at 400°F for 10 minutes or until barely colored. Cool before serving, dusted with a little confectioners' sugar.

Mint Tea

Atay bel na'na'

The making of mint tea in Morocco is steeped in ritual, and it is usually the master of the house who is responsible for preparing and serving it. A good mint tea will always be sweetened with pieces of sugar hacked from a cane sugar loaf, which comes wrapped in gorgeous purple tissue paper, and the sugar is added to the pot rather than to individual cups. If you prefer, the sugar can be omitted or the quantity reduced, or you can use an artificial sweetener. **Serves 4**

2 teaspoons green tea leaves

3 tablespoons sugar

1½ cups sprigs of fresh mint

1 Rinse the teapot with boiling water, then put in the tea leaves. Add a little boiling water and swirl it around before carefully pouring the water out, leaving the tea leaves in the pot.

2 Fill the pot with boiling water (about 3¼ cups) and stir in the sugar. Crush the mint a little with your hands, then add to the pot. Push the mint down into the liquid with a spoon. Leave to infuse for 2–3 minutes. Serve in traditional tea glasses or tea cups.

Pomegranate Juice

'Asseer del Rumman

Fresh juices like this are very popular in Morocco, and the juice-sellers on the streets all have a large metal citrus press with a strong lever, which does the job of extracting the juice in seconds. Pomegranates range in color from a delicate pearly pink to a bright red, depending on the variety. Make sure you buy sweet pomegranates and not the sour ones that are used in cooking. Pomegranates are also dried for use in infusions to soothe a stomach ache, as well as being used to dye wool yellow. **Serves 4–6**

1 Extract the juice from the pomegranates. There are two ways to do this. The quickest is to cut the fruits in half and press them like oranges. This can be a little messy, especially if you are using a domestic press where you hold the fruit down by hand; some seeds will fall out which will have to be pressed with your fingers. Also, the pressed juice may have a hint of bitterness, from the acrid inside flesh. The other method, which will produce more and finer juice, is to ease out the seeds, which you then put through a vegetable juicer, but you will need patience as it is time-consuming.

2 Pour the juice into a pitcher and stir in the orange flower water. If you are not going to serve the juice straight away, make sure you cover it well so that it does not oxidize.

5 large, juicy sweet pomegranates (about 4½ pounds) *slightly chilled*

5 teaspoons orange flower water, or to taste

121

Fresh Grape and Beet Juices

'Asseer del Zbib/'Asseer del Barba

To dazzle your family and friends, serve pitchers of these juices together. The strong colors of pistachio-green grape juice and blood-red beet juice look sumptuous next to each other.
Serves 4

2¾ pounds green seedless grapes *slightly chilled*

2–3 teaspoons orange flower water

Grape Juice

1 Pick the grapes off the stems, and process them through a vegetable juicer. You should have about 3 cups juice.

2 Add the orange flower water to taste and serve. If you want to make the juice ahead of time, keep it in an airtight container so that it does not oxidize. Stir well before serving, as grape juice separates very quickly.

2¾ pounds raw beets *chilled and cut into chunks*

4 teaspoons orange flower water, or to taste

¼ teaspoon ground cinnamon

Beet Juice

1 Process the beets in a vegetable juicer to yield about 3½ cups juice.

2 Add the orange flower water and ground cinnamon, and stir well until the cinnamon is completely blended.

Almond Milk

Hleeb del lawz

I loved the Italian almond drink crema di mandorle—*until I tried the Moroccan version. Whereas the Italian drink is slightly thin and has a hint of bitterness,* Hleeb del lawz *is lusciously rich and creamy with a fragrant taste. It makes a delightful non-alcoholic summer drink. If you find it too rich or too sweet, dilute it with more water.*
Serves 4

1 Soak the almonds in boiling water for 15–20 minutes. Drain well and put in a food processor. Add the sugar and process until you have a very fine paste.

2 Transfer the almond paste to a mixing bowl (preferably one with a spout) and pour in 2½ cups water. Stir until the paste is diluted and the sugar has completely dissolved. Leave to infuse in the refrigerator for 30 minutes or longer.

3 Strain into a pitcher through a very fine sieve (if you don't have one, line your colander with cheesecloth), pressing on the almond pulp to extract as much liquid as you can. Discard the almond pulp. Stir the orange flower water into the almond milk. Taste and adjust the drink to your liking. Serve chilled.

2 cups blanched almonds

½ cup sugar

1 tablespoon orange flower water, or to taste

I wish to thank the following for their help: Mr. El Kasmi and Leila Boubia at the Moroccan Tourist Office for organizing my accommodation during my last trip to Morocco; Philippe de Vizcaya at the Minza Hotel, Tangiers; Hakima Benkirane at the Rabat Hilton; Tonino Stabile at the Royal Mansour, Casablanca; the *directeur général* at Villa Maroc, Essaouira; Hassan Fuad at the Tishka and Pierre Bergé at the Mammounia, Marrakesh, for their generous hospitality.

I am also indebted to Boujemaa Mars, the head chef at the Mammounia, for showing me around his kitchens and giving me recipes; to Aln'quir Alhaj Almustapha ben Alhaj Omar who initiated me in the secrets of preparing and baking *mechouis* and showed me where to shop for the finest spices; to Mr. Chami at the Stellia restaurant in Marrakesh for inviting me to two spectacular meals; to Hassan, the *sous-chef* at El Korsan at the Minza for taking the time to talk to me about various street and regional dishes.

Furthermore, I would like to express my gratitude to Mina Hamouchi in Italy and her family in Morocco: Leila, Fatima, and Abdellah Filali, Moha and Khadija Khettouch and their children, and sisters Suad and Fatiha, who all received me as one of theirs and gave me wonderful family recipes. I am also grateful to Myriam Aherdane in Rabat for inviting me to her beautiful home and giving me the best *mechoui* I have ever tasted; to Jaouad Dich and Khadija Labbouh and her family in Tetouan; Farida Jehlil in Fez; Souad Meziane in Casablanca; Boubkir Temli and his brothers and Amal Al-Sabah in Tangiers, as well as Rashid my guide there and Hassan, my guide in Fez.

I would like to thank the following for testing some of the recipes in this book: Richard Hosking, Peter Fuhrman, and Vippy Rangsit, Allegra Mostyn-Owen and Daniel Jeffreys, Liz Walker, my sister Marie Karam, and Catey Hillier. I am also beholden to the following friends for letting me use their kitchens instead of my own cluttered one: Clare and James Kirkman, Peregrine and Patricia Pollen (who also tested recipes for me), Leine and Simon Watson, my sister again, and Caroline Davidson, my agent and friend, whose children Emma and Robert and au pair Odile Cornuz have been wonderful *sous-chefs*.

Finally, I would like to thank Ilaria Borletti and my brother Joseph Helou for their constant support; Alan Davidson and Helen Sabeni for all their help with my research, and Jenni Muir, Suzannah Gough, and Kate Bell at Conran Octopus, as well as Norma MacMillan and Meg Jansz. Last but not least, I would like to apologize to those who have helped me and whom I have forgotten to mention.